Et Tu, Cavapoo?

to George + Karen,

Et Tu, Cavapoo?

A DOG'S LIFE IN ROME

clear,

MARK RADCLIFFE

WITH ILLUSTRATIONS BY BELLA RADCLIFFE

corsair

CORSAIR

First published in Great Britain in 2025 by Corsair

1 3 5 7 9 10 8 6 4 2

Copyright © Mark Radcliffe, 2025
Illustrations copyright © Bella Radcliffe, 2025

The moral right of the author has been asserted.

A CIP catalogue record for this book
is available from the British Library.

Hardback ISBN: 978-1-4721-6034-8

Typeset in Sabon and Candara by M Rules
Printed and bound in Great Britain by
Clays Ltd, Elcograf S.p.A.

Papers used by Corsair are from well-managed forests
and other responsible sources.

MIX
Paper | Supporting
responsible forestry
FSC
www.fsc.org   FSC® C104740

Corsair
An imprint of
Little, Brown Book Group
Carmelite House
50 Victoria Embankment
London EC4Y 0DZ

The authorised representative
in the EEA is
Hachette Ireland
8 Castlecourt Centre
Dublin 15, D15 XTP3, Ireland
(email: info@hbgi.ie)

An Hachette UK Company
www.hachette.co.uk

www.littlebrown.co.uk

*To the greatest city in the world
and dog lovers everywhere*

Introduction

'Me and Him walking past a big dish of water.'

Call me Arlo. Some months ago, never mind how long precisely, having little or no money in my purse and nothing particular to interest me at home, I thought I would travel about a little and see the Roman part of the world.

Call me Mark. Arlo is my dog: a cavapoo from Kendal who was the only butterscotch-coloured one in a litter of pure black siblings. He's five years old at time of writing and it's fair to say that he and I are unhealthily co-dependent to the extent that I'm pretty sure I know what he would want to say if he could speak. It's the way he cocks his head on one side when I'm talking to him that tells me he's quite capable of understanding not only words like 'ball' and 'sit' but also full sentences such as:

'Would you like to go to the beach today?'

He sits on my knee in the kitchen when I read the paper and accompanies me whenever I go to the pub. If I put my coat on, he hangs around by the front door to make it tricky for me to go anywhere without him. Which I don't much. One look from that little furry face and he's got me.

Having said that, his knowledge of the opening of *Moby Dick* is surprising. He's not an avid reader and certainly doesn't have a clear understanding of time or financial independence. He also seems perfectly happy at home, but I feel respect is due for how closely he has stuck to the original text.

So how did we get here?

In March 2024, I decided to take time out from my less than hectic broadcasting schedule to live in Rome for a few months. I'm perfectly happy at home, too, but there is one place where I felt an immediate connection, almost as if I'd lived there before in a previous life. Not that I have much truck with the concept of reincarnation. Everyone who believes in it seems to think they've passed this way before as an Amazon queen, Aztec overlord or Voodoo witchdoctor. No one ever thinks they were previously a serf digging latrines. Or a slug.

Anyway, the locale in question is the district of Rome called Trastevere.

The first time I visited the Italian capital was in 1997. My radio sidekick Marc 'Lard' Riley and I were in the final painful days of seeing out the mercy killing of our Radio 1 breakfast show which, when we took it over, had the biggest listenership in Europe. Well, not for long.

As a last hurrah, thanks to the benevolence of our managers, who'd really had no choice but to let us go given the tumbling audience ratings, we'd been allowed to broadcast from the Italian capital as the England football team were on the brink of qualifying for the World Cup. They duly did so after an attritional 0–0 draw at the Stadio Olimpico on 11 October. You may remember the famous pictures of that game featuring a battle-scarred Paul Ince wearing a bloodstained headband, having received stitches to a gash before returning to see the match out. What a guy!

Afterwards, we freakishly managed to hail a taxi despite being in the midst of several thousand disgruntled and distinctly Anglophobic Azzurri fans trudging back to the city centre. When the driver asked where we wanted to go, we suddenly realised we didn't really know. Fortunately my wife, Bella, who speaks Italian having lived in Rome for a year as a young au pair, directed him to Trastevere. There, a magical world opened up.

Essentially it is a warren of narrow, deliciously distressed cobbled streets radiating from the Piazza di Santa Maria in the centre and the Piazza Trilussa at the other end, by the river. Here you will find myriad buzzing bars, time-warped trattoria and gaily coloured gelato galleria swamped by a constant stream of visitors. The soft light and the faded pinks, yellows and oranges of the peeling walls make it almost resemble a film set, and so it is no surprise to discover that Sergio Leone and Ennio Morricone went to school together there. The atmosphere of the place has to have fed into their iconic collaborations somehow. On Via Gloriosa you can see a plaque indicating the location of Sergio Leone's childhood home. It looks like a modest apartment in an unremarkable block, though it will still likely set you back the best part of half a million quid now. You can also still visit his favourite restaurant, Checco Er Carettiere, where a school photograph of Sergio with Morricone and the owner, Francisco Porcecci, hangs on the wall. Federico Fellini ate there too. There's also a picture of a dinner in 1982 with Leone, Robert De Niro, Gabriel García Márquez and Muhammad Ali. You would have to say that that is an A-list table.

Oh, a tip. If you're on a budget, go round the back of the eating house. They have a takeaway window there and some metal chairs and tables. You'll get your Sergio Leone memorial carbonara for about six or seven quid.

Trastevere literally means 'beyond the Tiber' as it is on the other side of the river from the walled city and the heavyweight sightseer spots on the tourist trail, like the Colosseum, Pantheon, Spanish Steps and Trevi Fountain. If you cross over the Bridge of

Angels and turn left at the Castel Sant' Angelo you're about a ten-to-fifteen-minute walk away. Alternatively traverse via Tiber Island and you're more or less right there.

Throughout its history, the district has had that sense of 'otherness' about it. It has perpetually hovered in the hinterland between Left Bank chic and the wrong side of the tracks. Of course, it has changed even during my time of visiting. In 1997 it was thronging with locals. Tourists not so much. Everybody knows about it now, but its character, its atmosphere, its heart remain intact. And crucially, it doesn't try too hard to please. It is pretty but not pristine; desirable yet dishevelled. There are people dressed in mismatched clothes with agricultural hairstyles, but I get the impression they are what they are, not what they're trying to be. That's the essence of Trastevere.

And so, with that later life sense of freedom that came with my parents having passed away and the kids grown up, it seemed a good time to visit for an extended period.

So it was that Arlo, Bella and I set off on a road trip in our VW Beetle convertible to take us there via a lazy meander through several European destinations that seemed like they might be pleasant stop-offs.

Prior to departure, I had to make sure all Arlo's paperwork was in order. After his rabies jab a month in advance I had to obtain his pet passport. I thought this was going to be a cutesy smaller version of my own with perhaps a paw print or something embossed on the laminated cover and an adorable photo of him inside. Imagine my disappointment to find out it was two sheets of A4 paper stapled together. At a cost of £200. Now, my own newly renewed permit is valid for ten years and, as I did it online, the price was £88.50. Arlo's was valid for ninety days. Do the maths. Actually, I've done it for you. Pro rata my document costs £2.10 for ninety days so his was one hundred times more expensive. Does that sound fair to you? No, me neither.

Packing the car proved interesting as the boot space in a Beetle is limited, although we were confident that going away for three months essentially meant packing for a week and washing stuff every seven days or so. Of course, this calculation did not allow for how many daily changes you need to make as an habitué of the temperate North Country when inhabiting warmer climes. Still, it's not illegal to gently reek, is it? It's only temporary. They do have showers over there.

Arlo's luggage was minimal, though I did insist on packing a large sack of his preferred food just in case we couldn't source it in Rome. Bella told me this was ridiculous but I was pretty sure I'd be proved right when this particular brand became notable by its absence at journey's end. Perhaps, then, you can imagine the conversation that ensued when we discovered it was in stock at a pet shop in the next street to our rented apartment.

Space issues aside, we love our Beetle convertible. Not that we have the roof down much. I would but Bella and Arlo, who both have considerably more hair than me, don't particularly enjoy it. Arlo puts on his grumpy face and hunkers as far down into his travel basket as he can, looking at me as if I am an idiot. I know exactly what he's thinking.

If you can be warm and cosy in a car why spoil it by taking the roof off?

Put like that, he's got a point and I was usually outvoted two to one. In three months in Europe, I think we had the top down three times.

Arlo absolutely prioritises his own comfort. He's been known to unwrap folded throws to give himself a softer berth on the sofa. He's happy to drink out of a muddy puddle but otherwise loathes water. Even a warm, soapy bath enriched with overpriced canine unguents. His attitude to water is simple:

Why be wet when you could be dry?

Again, for the most part, he's got a point.

Having shuttled across the Channel, we first went to Reims, where Claude Monet got a bit obsessed with the facade of the cathedral. It is pretty impressive to be fair.

Next was Strasbourg, which I'd expected to be sleek and modernist as all I knew of it was the European Parliament building. What a surprise then to find a fairy-tale city of medieval buildings, narrow streets and waterways. You felt like you could turn a corner and glimpse Baron Bomburst's castle in *Chitty Chitty Bang Bang*.

Next was Lucerne, which was pretty and we had a lovely sail on the lake but it was expensive. I mean, £25 for a baked potato? Switzerland, you're having a laugh!

From there it was on to charming Bellagio on Lake Como, which I thought might be a bit Riviera posey and overpriced. It wasn't.

And so to our final port-of-call, which was the impressive and impressively busy Bologna. Where I had bolognese. When in Rome.

What follows is in no sense a guide book but rather a record of our Roman ramblings, in both senses of the word, as seen by me and Arlo. He can't speak, as we've established. He's a dog. But I know that when he tilts his head that way and listens to me, he is taking it all in and so I'm confident that this was what was going on inside his head.

Which is quite small.

About the size of a grapefruit.

SPQR-lo! Salve Roma!

So here we are in Rome. I know we must be here because all the bags are out of the car. I hate bags. Whenever I see suitcases in the hallway at home I start to panic in case They're going somewhere and I'm not.

Over the past week we've been sleeping in a different little house every night even though I'm not really sure how many years a week is. Every morning, I've been watching Her and Him pack bags again and wondering if I'm going to be left sitting on the bed. I haven't been so far but you never know. I'm keeping my eye on them and no mistake.

When we got to a big place with lots of humans and buildings it seemed really noisy because lots of inconsiderate people were ringing bells all over town. Come on, guys, have some consideration. It's Sunday, for heaven's sake. Everybody wants a bit of peace and quiet.

Anyway, we're now in a funny small house with no garden up about a thousand steps. Perhaps these are the Spanish Steps I've heard them talk about.

They weren't. These were just the steps up to our apartment, which numbered about thirty. Arlo's default expression is wide-eyed as his little beady peepers stare unblinkingly through his lustrous eyebrows. This makes him appear as if he's looking at the world with a sense of wonder and is therefore prone to exaggeration. To be fair, stairs are not a big part of his life in Cheshire. He does get very nervous at the sight of luggage, though, so the week of travelling must have been kind of stressful for him. Every time we checked into another hotel he would have been thinking:

Ah right, so we live here now.

To be honest, I think he would have been happy in any of those places except that peculiarly cell-like room on the outskirts of Lucerne. I don't think he fancied living there. I certainly didn't.

We arrived in Rome on a Sunday to a chorus of church bells as the faithful made their way to one of the city's 930 places of worship. Arlo is, I think, both undecided and unengaged with the existence, or not, of a higher power, which makes him something of a dognostic. Nevertheless it seemed rather unfair that he wasn't going to be allowed into any of the churches we were going to visit. Accepting the omnipotence of the Almighty, for argument's sake, aren't we all God's creations?

How does that hymn go?

All things bright and beautiful, all creatures great and small,
All things wise and wonderful, the Lord God made them all.

So here's my question on behalf of Arlo and his kind:

If this 'Lord God' made us all, then why are only some of 'us all' allowed in his 'house'?

Seems a bit judgemental, right? Then again there are certain practicalities to be taken into consideration. While reading up on which public gardens in Rome were canine friendly, I stumbled upon a forum on which the following question appeared:

'Can you take your dog into the Sistine Chapel?'

I mean, think about what you're saying. The Sistine Chapel is located within the sprawling enclosed labyrinth of the Vatican Museums. What happens if, after several hours perusing the ravishing Raphael Rooms and the wondrous Gallery of Maps, you arrive under Michelangelo's masterpiece only for your golden retriever to squat and leave an offering the Lord would not appreciate? Come on, guys, think it through.

However, Arlo's exclusion has brought us up against one of the central dichotomies of organised religion. Are all welcome or not? 'Good will to all men (and dogs)' is something most of us will happily sign up to, but within the context of multiple faiths this hinges on tolerance and acceptance among all denominations. How's that gone then?

The Cat Colony of Area Sacra di Largo Argentina

'Me and a stupid cat at a building site.'

Today we strolled to a dusty square where some bits of pillars were sticking up out of the ground among some piles of bricks and stones and stuff. Not much to see here. Like a building site. Except there were loads and loads of quite manky-looking cats lolling around on the rubble behind a see-through barrier.

Now, I'm a laid-back kind of guy, except when it comes to posties, swans, squirrels ...

When I'm chasing squirrels, I have a special yelp that I only use on those occasions. They run away like the clappers and they are right to do so because I'm a bit of a tough nut when roused. I have a different bark to warn off those hissing swans but they're safe from me as they're behind railings on the pond at home in a different country that I think might be in a different world.

And the postman? I really give him what for. No wonder he leaves the letters and parcels in that cupboard outside. If he put his fingers through that little flap in the door I'd give them a nip for sure. Actually, I probably wouldn't as I'm not really like that and I can't reach that little flap anyway. I tear up the first letter that drops on the doormat instead. That shows 'em.

Oh, and I hate cats of course. I am a dog, after all. I didn't make the rules. It was well frustrating at this place. All these cats were just like totally taunting me because they knew full well I couldn't get at them. Annoying or what? I could have cleared that place in seconds. I know my strengths. I keep our garden at home clear of posties, swans, squirrels and cats, and I could have got rid of this motley moggy crew in no time.

Poor Arlo. He was desperate to get at these undomesticated kitties and nearly tugged my arm off in his desire to find a way to reach them. Perhaps if he understood the historical significance of the place he might have paused for reflection. I did bend down and look him square in the face before proclaiming the phrase: 'Et tu, Arlo.' Because, while he may have been unimpressed by the 'stones and stuff', these 'bits of pillars' mark a place of great significance.

Here at the Sacra di Largo Argentina are the remains of four temples together with part of the curia (meeting rooms) of the Theatre of Pompey. The Senate used to meet here and on this very spot Julius Caesar was stabbed to death on the Ides of March (the 15th) in 44 BC. Of all the famous Roman incidents documented in history this might well be the most widely known. I can't help thinking that calling this place 'the cat colony' is focusing on the wrong thing really. Perhaps whoever initiated that plan had visited with their dog, too. If Brutus had had a cavapoo pulling him in the direction of the cats that day, the outcome for Caesar could have been very different.

Also, it's worth bearing in mind if you're thinking about coming to Rome that if you're as unimpressed as Arlo with 'bits of pillars' and 'piles of bricks and stones and stuff', it might not be the place for you. There's a lot of that and you might find yourself quite disappointed by the Forum.

The cat colony is in fact a long-standing sanctuary for the city's feral felines. They are watched over and cared for by a local charitable trust and you can adopt one if you like, though you can't take it home with you, obviously. The cats seem to have a pretty perfect life lounging about on the old stone slabs, being fed regularly and protected by a Plexiglas wall from would-be assailants like a certain cavapoo from the Lake District.

I reluctantly accept that my canine companion is not always going to be overly receptive to historical matters. This is a shame because, in a way, he has a part in this epic story. All dogs are supposed to share 99 per cent of their DNA with wolves, and one wolf in particular plays an important role in the legend of the foundation of Rome, having nurtured Romulus and Remus. We'll come to that.

It's really hard to think this genetic make-up is accurate in the case of Arlo, but if he is even 1 per cent lupine then it certainly kicks in when he sees a squirrel, postal worker, swan or cat, so this was clearly a highly frustrating experience for him. He somehow managed to regain his composure in due course, though, and as a token act of rebellion urinated copiously on the protective barricade.

He's right about our garden in Knutsford. He has carefully monitored the presence of any cats and squirrels and chased them off. We actually don't get many swans in there, so that boast is rather harder to verify, but it's worth bearing in mind that when St Patrick was despatched by Pope Celestine to be patron saint of Ireland, one of his jobs was to get rid of all the snakes. The thing is that there weren't any snakes in post-glacial times on the Emerald Isle so, you know, Arlo's not alone in bigging himself up without any real justification. Still, even though I'm on his side, you'd have to say that he is overestimating his pest-control abilities when considering the job at hand in our garden to be on a par with that in Rome. Rome's a lot bigger for a start, but then, how would he know that?

That night, as he curled up asleep on the cosy travelling rug he'd adopted, he twitched, chuffed and snorted. What was he dreaming about? Caesar, stray cats, the Roman Empire or squirrels?

He opened one droopy eye and looked at me. It was squirrels.

Cars

I used to live in a place called Knutsford but I've forgotten all about that now because I can't remember things for more than a period of time I have no way of measuring.

Rome is a lot busier than that town I was just talking about whose name escapes me now. There are millions of cars everywhere and they seem to park so close together that you wonder how people get out of them. Maybe they come through the sunroof or the hatchback.

I'm not sure where our car is but we don't seem to be using it. The last time I saw it was in a cave thing and someone took the keys off us and drove it away. I wonder if Him and Her have hit on hard times and so have had to sell it to that little bloke who lives with all his cars underground. I mean, how many cars does one person need?

Anyway, it suits me because now we just walk everywhere. Apart from waiting for some little humans to turn green we can go where we want whenever we want. If only there weren't so many motor vehicles it would be brilliant. Maybe there should be more of those funny little underground people who keep lots of them, like that bloke who bought ours. That would keep the streets clearer. I think I could have a go at barking most of them out of the way but it looks like that might be quite a dangerous thing to do as they're going quite fast. It's a thin line between bravery and stupidity, isn't it?

It is, and it's called a lead.

Knutsford came back to Arlo in seconds once he'd smelled it all again but he's right, Rome is full of cars. For obvious reasons, public transport in the centre of the Eternal City is limited. The buses are okay but every time they try and lay tram tracks or dig to extend the Metro they come across more 'bits of pillars and piles of stones' and have to abandon progress while the archaeologists move in.

So there are literally millions of scooters. Many are classic Lambrettas and Vespas but there are also lots of those that you pick up on an app and then leave strewn haphazardly across the pavement as a trip hazard to pedestrians and their dogs.

And there are hundreds of thousands of cars. Like ours, some are stored in subterranean garages with valet service, but most people just have to take their chances at street level. How anyone ever finds a parking space is a mystery as there don't seem to be any free, ever.

Roman cars are very different to those you see in the UK. They're generally tiny, the smaller the better for obvious reasons in a crowded city. Most of the makes and models are familiar to the UK motorist, but in contrast to their British counterparts, they are nearly all filthy and bear their dents and scratches proudly like battle scars. Cars here seem to be regarded in the same way as bins: necessary but not worth keeping in pristine condition. Or maybe central heating boilers. Taken for granted until they break down. I find this refreshing and logical. Have a crappy car, then it doesn't matter if it gets crappier. What a welcome contrast to the British and their worship of ever-more ludicrously outsized SUVs kept spotlessly polished.

Nor do the Italians, with their noted sense of style, succumb to the ultimate badge of motoring idiocy that is the personalised number plate. You know, guys, I had my name in my clothes at school but I grew out of it. Think about the kind of person you've become.

The Italians do have illustrious history when it comes to automotive design. Companies like Ferrari, Maserati, Bugatti and Lamborghini are all manufacturers of iconic and much coveted classics. You don't really see these on the streets of Rome as they would be scraped in seconds by an antediluvian Fiat 126 covered in bird droppings with only one functioning rear light and an off-side front wing held on with gaffer tape.

It's also worth noting that Ferruccio Lamborghini started out in 1948 making tractors before cars, and this proud agricultural tradition is alive and well in Roman motorists' approach to driving, parking and vehicle appearance. I love it. I mean what really is the point of cleaning a car? It will get dirty again. You don't clean your bin, do you? Oh, you do? Have you got a personalised number plate?

Actually, I could be accused of hypocrisy here. I did once disinfect our wheelie bin. That was ten minutes I'll never get back. Arlo was with me the whole time but keeping a safe distance so as not to be too close to his despised H_2O. He twisted his head right over to look at me almost sideways and I could feel his disdain.

'Washing the bins,' he was thinking. 'Who cares if a bin smells?'

I guess I do, a bit. He doesn't. Just the opposite. Dogs are the best creatures on earth but they do love a rank odour. How can you not like a foamy bath but relish rolling in toxic fox poo?

Also, I do have the car cleaned twice a year whether it needs it or not, and respect is due to Kev, Nathan and Ryan at Autoden, who valeted the Beetle before we set off.

As Arlo rightly observes, it is a bit of a mystery how close together cars are parked in Rome. It often looks impossible for the driver to have had enough room to get out. Perhaps he's right and they do exit through the sunroof or climb through the hatchback. This seems to me a pretty good idea. Imagine how closely you could park, nose in, if you didn't need to open doors on the sides. Is there another way either vertically or through the rear-end of effecting ingress and egress from our vehicles? Either that or, in an age where driverless cars are a reality, don't we have the technology to make the wheels turn sidewise so you could just move directly into a space without all that reverse-parking nonsense? You know, like castors? Come on, Elon. Get it together.

Some vehicles on the streets of the city appear not to have moved for months or even years judging by the dust, rust and crust caked on them. This makes sense, I suppose. You don't want to take your car out and lose your parking space, do you?

In England these days, most drivers are pretty good at letting you cross the road at a zebra crossing and fairly observant when using their indicators. Rather like the personalised number plate brigade, those drivers who don't use their indicators are deserving of contempt. Who can't be bothered to move their hand from there to there? A distance of about an inch. Idiots.

In Rome, there doesn't seem to be a hard-and-fast rule about stopping to let pedestrians walk over a crossing. Sometimes they do, sometimes they don't. Within the reasonable bounds of safety you've just got to go for it. Nonchalantly, of course. You don't want them thinking they've got you worried.

And absolutely nobody ever indicates, which is clearly viewed as an affectation. I suppose, to be fair, you've only got two hands and you're utilising those already: one on the steering wheel and the other to hold your phone, which everyone routinely uses while driving. You would have thought with their deep-rooted love of the extravagant gesture that hands-free systems would be commonplace, but not so, mystifyingly.

The Elephant and Obelisk of Gian Lorenzo Bernini

Today we saw an elephant. I know what elephants are because I saw some on the big box with pictures on it that sits in the corner of the room at home. So the ones that I've seen were normal-sized, something like a gerbil, but this one was massive. Weirdly it's got a big spike sticking out of its back. What's that all about then?

There were lots of people looking at this deformed animal including some waving folded-up umbrellas and little flags on sticks and talking ten to the dozen. Wow, calm down, people. Enough already. It's just an elephant. And not even a real one I don't think. At least it didn't move while I was there. Maybe it's just some kind of ornament. Maybe somebody famous made it or something. Anyway, whoever made it can't have been all that good because the trunk looks a bit long to me.

Having a lovely time, although they don't seem to have my favourite corned beef here.

Arlo really loves corned beef, of which there is an Italian variant called *carne salada*. Not that we found any in the local shops, so he had to make do with pancetta. He approached it with caution initially. Unlike most dogs, who nearly take your hand off when offered a titbit, Arlo approaches at his usual stately, unhurried pace and cautiously inhales to make sure the offering is up to his regal standards. He's the only dog I know who rejects sausages.

The elephant he's talking about is in the Piazza della Minerva and it's about a quarter of the size of a real elephant, I would say. But to be fair to Arlo, if you'd only ever seen elephants on a television screen, how would you know they weren't gerbil-sized in real life?

He's also heading down the right track when he wonders if someone famous created it. They did. It's by Gian Lorenzo Bernini (1598–1680) who was the undisputed guvnor of the Baroque sculpture scene in Rome and was generally thought to be the natural heir to Michelangelo. Not content with being the Grana Padano of the statue scene, though, he was also a painter, playwright, actor and architect. Indeed, it is his design that greets you when you approach the piazza and basilica of St Peter. His works, masterpieces all, are dotted throughout the city. If you want to check out some of his best creations then nip along to the church of San Sebastiano, above some pretty cool catacombs, where you can see his transcendental final sculpture: *Salvator Mundi* – a bust of the Saviour. It would be a miracle to achieve that with pencil or paint let alone with a hammer and chisel on a block of marble. It just makes you gape in wonder. And he was eighty when he made it. No early retirement in those days evidently. Genius though Bernini undoubtedly was, I think Arlo has a good eye. I think the trunk is a bit long as well. It's probably a bit late to change it now though.

Bernini is everywhere in Rome. You can even see his cute first autographed work in the Galleria Borghese. It's called *The Goat Amathea with Infant Jupiter and Faun*. Snappy title, eh?

I also really like his *Damned Soul* in the Palazzo di Spagna. It was made in 1619 yet looks oddly contemporary (and a bit like Donald Sutherland).

Hey, perhaps looking at sculpture in museums and churches isn't your thing, but you don't need to do that to appreciate

Bernini's genius. Head to the Piazza Navona, where you can't miss his Fountain of the Four Rivers. It's a bit ostentatious for my taste but you'll get the drift of what he was all about. Arlo, with a bit of gentle persuasion and being cradled by the rim of its pool, had a drink out of it and thereby makes a notable point. All this stuff is fancy beyond imagination but, at the end of the day, it's a fountain and dogs need to drink. Even the masters of the Baroque had to consider practicality.

And while we're on Bernini, can we just raise the matter of a major slur against his legacy? Leonardo, Michelangelo, Raphael? Fair enough. But how did Donatello get in ahead of Bernini when it came to naming the Teenage Mutant Ninja Turtles? It's an outrage.

Oh, and the people waving umbrellas and little flags are local guides. There are lots of them ambling about, droning on and on and on ad nauseam. I know they need to make a living but why on earth would you hire one? How much do you really need to know about an elephant statue? How long would you ideally like the information to last? A minute? Ninety seconds? These professional motormouths bleat on for absolutely ages to justify what you're paying them. By the time they've given you the full quarter of an hour, you've completely glazed over and have forgotten nearly everything you've been told. Your mind has wandered on to other things like Aperol spritz and cold beer. Cut to the chase, tour guides. Give us the bare bones. We can always go online later.

I observed one family being bombarded with stone non-ruminant ungulate information for a good twenty minutes. The teenage boy of the group, wearing a Slipknot hoodie, looked like he'd rather be undergoing root-canal surgery, but then I guess some people would rather undergo root-canal surgery than listen to Slipknot.

The Colosseum and Queues

I don't look up all that much when I'm out and about. I was built close to the ground for a reason – so I can easily smell stuff. Rome is nice and whiffy although not excessively so. I was a bit disappointed, in truth. I really thought it would stink. No fox poo so far, more's the pity.

If I do glance up it seems like someone has been drawing on all the walls. She draws and paints a lot. Perhaps it was Her.

Another thing that takes some getting used to is people standing in lines getting in the way of the places I want to sniff. I didn't have this problem when I used to live in that other place that I've forgotten all about now. Some of these fools seem to be queueing up for food in houses with lots of tables and chairs in them. But then there are lots of other houses with chairs and tables with no people in them at all so why don't they just go there? Imagine queueing up for food. Crazy. When I go to my dish there's only me there. Brilliant. What's on the menu today then? I hope it's not pancetta again.

There were really massive queues to get into a big pile of stones that had partially fallen down. Apparently they used to kill a lot of animals there so I was keen to get inside and right a few wrongs. I'm told that a while ago, maybe last week, one idiot killed a hundred lions in a single day. I'm not surprised. Like elephants, I've seen lions on the telly and they're about gerbil-sized as well. They didn't stand a chance. Pick on someone your own size, idiot.

Actually, it turned out dogs weren't allowed in there. Oh well, at least there's the Sistine Chapel to look forward to.

Yes, it seemed unkind to explain to him that he wasn't going to go there either after his disappointment at being refused entry to the Colosseum. He's correct to say that parts of it have crumbled, but there are quite a lot of good bits left.

Of course, everyone is familiar with the Colosseum and all the bloodletting that went on there in the name of sport. A bit like boxing today but with more wild animals. But if you want to get a real flavour of how things unfolded then, check out the recent documentary *Gladiator II* in which Paul Mescal plays the part of a real-life Roman heavyweight champion called Russell Crowe.

The mass big-cat butchery did take place but considerably longer ago than Arlo's estimate. These were the idiotic antics of antiquity committed by the Emperor Commodus, who was a real piece of work when it came to culling proud beasts for a laugh. He was in office from AD 177 to 192 and did indeed kill a hundred lions in a day. However, he had no real understanding of showbiz. He followed that orgy of slaughter by decapitating an ostrich. You want to look at your running order there, mate. After all those lions, do you really think one solitary ostrich constitutes a grand finale?

Commodus was assassinated in 192 by a group that included members of his own brood. Quite the family fallout. I guess it was a bit like an ancient Roman edition of *The Jeremy Kyle Show*. Interesting to note that, rather like the public displays of wanton cruelty once staged at the Colosseum have been consigned to the past, so has Jeremy Kyle's television show. Reassuring to know that civilisation marches ever onwards.

I did look Commodus up and discovered that he was remembered as 'cruel, erratic and lecherous'. However, it also states that 'he wasn't a bad Emperor in every respect', which probably means he sorted out the sewers, although he doesn't appear to have invented the commode, sadly.

I was as surprised as Arlo that the city wasn't more of an olfactory assault but perhaps if we'd been there in high summer, when temperatures can reach forty degrees, things would have been different.

He's also right that there is a lot of graffiti in Trastevere and Rome in general. I think it adds to the atmosphere and general air of bohemianism but I know that not everyone will agree. Some people will pay multimillions for a Jean-Michel Basquiat painting while others think he should have had an ASBO. They do make token attempts to clean some of this stuff away but I find it really charming that the trucks that are sent round by the cleansing department to tackle the problem have themselves been skilfully and garishly tagged by the graffiti artists. And they look better for it.

Rome's graffiti artists could be said to be the latest exponents of an art as old as the city itself. Outside many churches and public buildings, you will find fragments of stone with names, messages and even the odd cartoon chiselled into them. These are early examples of a kind of graffiti where pilgrims and travellers left a memento of their visit. I guess the coppers must have been slow back then as it would take you a lot longer to hammer your tag into a slab than whip out the aerosol paint can.

When he says 'Her' he means Bella, but I don't think she contributed to the phenomenon. Stylistically, it would be a radical departure from the line drawings in this book. Having said that, 'She' goes to bed about two hours later than me and Arlo so she could be up to anything, I suppose. Arlo and I get up earlier than

Bella so, when in Rome, we could have been up to anything, too. We weren't though. We walked round the Piazza di Santa Maria in Trastevere and then went to the Bar San Calisto for a croissant (shared) and a coffee (not).

The queueing thing is another feature of Roman life, and it's a bit hard to understand if you're not of the TikTok generation.

There's a restaurant, which has three branches in Trastevere, called Tonnarello. It's been a fixture of Roman dining since 1876 so they must be doing something right. There are huge queues outside all their outlets at all times. In fact, it can be off-putting having someone glare at you while you shovel in another mouthful of amatriciana as you know they are willing you to finish as fast as you can so they can have your seat. But here's the thing. The food in Tonnarello is classic Romagna pasta and pizza and it is great ... but it's equally great everywhere else. Go to a trattoria without a queue and the food will be just as good and you'll have saved yourself the best part of an hour.

In the centre of the city is a sandwich shop called All'antico Vinaio. There are two branches on opposite corners. The queues are without exaggeration often a hundred people long. Down the street I saw another sandwich bar selling more or less the same thing with only three people waiting. Now, I have to say that All'antico's butties were much bigger so my solution was not to wait for forty-five minutes but to go down the road to the other bap shop and buy two. Go on, knock yourself out.

Arlo enjoys eating out and Roman eateries proved dog-friendly to a degree I hadn't really expected. He was welcomed everywhere and, of course, has perfect table manners in that he sits quietly underneath and waits patiently for slivers of Parma ham or shavings of pecorino. If you ignore him for too long he might give you a little gruff to remind you that another amuse-bouche is overdue, but other than that, he's silent and still. I know there are people who say you shouldn't feed a dog from the table but how can you see that yearning hairy mug looking up at you and refuse him? If you can, you have a different relationship with the animal kingdom than me. Perhaps you're distantly related to Commodus.

There really shouldn't be any need to wait for food in Rome. It has thirteen thousand restaurants. That sounded like a lot to me so I looked up London, which has fifteen thousand. But the population of Rome is about three million – not much compared to England's capital, which has closer to nine million. These figures may be affected by tourist influx but I've decided to gloss over that as I'm a bloke writing a book about his dog and not the Office for National Statistics. So, my seasonally non-adjusted figures mean that there is a restaurant for every 600 people in the Smoke whereas in the Eternal City that figure drops to 230.

I also checked my closest city of Manchester. Greater Manchester's population is similar to that of Rome and yet there are only 650 restaurants. Can that be right? That would mean that for every food outlet in Cottonopolis there would potentially be 4,615 people. It's amazing we're not all suffering from malnutrition!

The Spanish Steps and Water

'Me thinking what it would be like with no
people on some steps that are Spanish.'

Today we went up yet more steps. Again about a thousand of them. What is it with steps here? Why hang around a crowded staircase when you could just go to a park? And not only that, we stopped at the bottom of the steps for absolutely ages looking up at a window.

I obviously had no choice about which humans I was going to live with and mostly They seem okay but I'm starting to wonder if They are perhaps a bit boring. I mean, whose idea of a good time is looking up at a window? Come on, guys, live a little.

Now, these steps actually are the famous Spanish ones apparently, although they're in Italy, designed by Italians and paid for by a French guy, as I somehow seem to know.

It was very hot and very crowded. I was actually pretty thirsty and even though you're never far from a kind of free tap thing in Rome, I find it a bit beneath me to slurp like the local dogs from a gushing torrent, so He usually carries around a little dish for me in that daft pouch thing He wears on holiday. However, He'd forgotten it today, the massive fool, and so we tried to get to what must be the Spanish Fountain at the bottom of the Spanish Steps. The crowds were too big, though, and we couldn't get anywhere near it so we had to go to one of the houses with lots of tables and buy water with money, for goodness' sake. Paying for water. That's mental. That'll teach Him to forget my dish.

Harsh but fair. I'm with Arlo on this. In Rome you can safely quaff the tap water and there are lots of drinking fountains on the street. And yet people seem determined to pay for it. With money.

I imagine they think it has greater purity because it's 'mineral' water. That's not necessarily true. It's generally in a plastic bottle for a start. Haven't you heard about the effect of plastic on our seas? What you've just paid for has got loads more crap in it than the stuff that's coming out of the mains. But sometimes you'll be paying for bottled water thinking it's fresh out of some natural torrent of youth when in fact it's out of the tap in the kitchen and here's how that happens. The waiter/waitress brings a branded bottle of water to the table. They show it to you and you nod. They then place their closed fist over the top of it and quickly twist. Did you hear the seal break? No. Because it didn't. It's a reused receptacle filled up in the kitchen. Now while this is environmentally sound, in a way, they're still making you pay for something that's essentially free (-ish). In this case, a small bottle cost me €3.50. Imagine how many times a day they do that at a busy café.

The solution? Always ask for tap water and if they refuse then turn the table over and storm off. I didn't do this, of course. I smiled meekly and paid. The waiter was a friendly and attentive chap. Even if he was a flagrant racketeer.

The Spanish Steps, of which there are 135 and not a thousand, are one of the 'must sees' on the tourist map. Sometimes Arlo surprises me with his historical knowledge even if he is sketchy on detail and unable to check things on a smartphone. I envy him that. He exists on a need-to-know basis. He lives in the moment and so on this occasion he was only concerned with miscounting steps and getting a drink. Now I think about it, I have human friends who operate on a similar basis.

But when an enquiring look crosses that petite hirsute visage I know he is sensing history. And he is right to question the veracity of the 'Spanish' tag. Francesco De Sanctis and Alessandro Specchi did the design and a French papal diplomat called Étienne Gueffier left some of his estate to fund construction when he died in 1660. It took them until 1723 to get started, though, which makes me wonder if, as part of the international effort, there wasn't some British involvement in an HS2 specialist delay consultancy sort of way.

So why Spanish then? you may well ask. Well, the steps lead from the Trinità dei Monti church at the top to the Piazza di Spagna at the foot, where the Spanish Embassy was once located. The Spanish have moved now. They got sick of the stairs. They've got a lift at their new place.

It's always crowded there unless you go really early. Bella's picture of Arlo in splendid isolation on the celebrated stairway is a somewhat idealised view. Sometimes you can barely see the steps themselves as so many people are lounging about on them. Interestingly, this is technically a municipal offence. There are signs, admittedly not very prominently positioned, letting you know the various things you're not allowed to do on this historic landmark and the fines you can therefore incur. If they fined everyone who squatted there they would make even more than flogging tap water. I was also fascinated to learn that according to Article 14 of the regulations of the Polizia Urbana, it is forbidden to 'shout, squall and sing'. So don't say you haven't been warned. Do your squalling somewhere else.

While you consider that, though, if you're as boring as us don't forget to at least glance up at the windows at the bottom right of the steps as you stand in the piazza. There you will see the sign telling you that the English poet John Keats died in an apartment here of tuberculosis aged just twenty-five on 23 February 1821. I did point this out to Arlo but he didn't seem unduly interested given that he was concentrating on not being trodden on by the mobs of unruly squallers flagrantly disregarding the local bylaws. He was also keen to get to the fountain at the bottom to guzzle on the free water. If only.

Oh, and this fountain is another Bernini masterpiece. It's a magnificently rendered boat called the Fontana della Barcaccia. When I say Bernini though, this isn't our old friend Gian Lorenzo but his dad, Pietro. So you could say that Gian was a real chip off the old block in perhaps the most apposite way it's possible to use that cliché.

St Peter's and the Vatican

'A building with a big bobble hat on.'

Today we walked along a very wide street that smelled mostly of meat. In the distance there seemed to be a big white building with a bobble hat on its head. There were a lot of people there in a very long line so if they were queueing up for food then I think they need more tables in the big bobble-hat house.

A funny thing happened when a odd-shaped little lady in black clothes got in my way but a nice man with no socks on – you tend to notice these things when you spend your life at human calf level – pushed her out of the way. Cheers, mate, although I think he could have done it a bit more politely.

There were also quite a lot of souvenirs with pictures of a bloke in a little white hat without a bobble on it for sale. They must really like this guy here. I don't know who he is but he might be called Frank. He has a kind face. I bet if I met him he would stroke me and maybe give me a treat. If you're reading this, bloke in little white hat, then I really like corned beef but a little bit of lovely smelly cheese is also acceptable.

He means the Pope, and the common way of addressing him is 'your Holiness'. I think you can move on to 'Frank' once you've been for pizza and a glass of Barolo.

The current pontiff is Jorge Mario Bergoglio. Better known as Pope Francis. He does have a nice face and looks like he might well stroke a dog and give it a treat (I'm pretty sure the 'lovely smelly cheese' Arlo has in mind is Gorgonzola) from a papal stash held in a secret pocket, which probably has a Latin name for it. Having said that, he has recently been highly critical of people having pets instead of children, and gave short shrift to a woman who wanted him to bless her pooch, so perhaps Arlo would have been disgruntled with his audience and turned to a different denomination. Dogs are pretty shallow like that.

You see Francis's face everywhere on a limitless range of generally quite tacky novelties, but then I suppose a lot of the faithful in Rome aren't exactly well off.

One of the souvenirs Arlo refers to is a plastic figurine of the Holy Father with a wobbling head on a spring. I bought one, of course. Mine was described as: 'The famous Pope Francis creazione Roya Bobbles Testoni Famosi Headknocker', which, we're reliably informed, is the 'Pope Francis bobblehead you've been hearing about'.

Oh right – THAT Pope Francis bobblehead.

Fascinated by the extent to which this had been a matter of global chitchat, I looked up some of the reviews of this item online. Someone called Ed claimed that: 'This bobblehead is of a much higher quality than I expected.' Oh come on, Ed. This is 'the famous headknocker that you've been hearing about'. How could you doubt the quality? Have a little faith.

Another satisfied customer was Margie, who said: 'Well, we all know that bobbleheads represent a particular character. The Pope's bobblehead does that in a respectful way.' Margie, you're so right. His head only bobbles a dignified amount. Too bobbly and it would be sacrilegious.

Maggie was equally content: 'Tis the era to own the bobblehead of the lovable present Pope. He is so down to earth I wouldn't be surprised if he'd choose this delightful image of himself for himself.' Awkwardly expressed, Maggie, but neither would I. I'm sure he nudged the nearest Swiss Guard and whispered: 'Oi – what's this bobblehead I've been hearing about? Nip out and get me one. Here's a €50 note and I want €16 change. I would like this delightful image of myself for myself. 'Tis the era, after all.'

'Tis, yes.

And true to his lowly and frugal roots he wanted his change. Good to know he keeps a tight rein on the pontifical purse strings. A Pope has to be financially astute. Take note, there is only one letter difference between Papal and PayPal.

Oddly, the approach to St Peter's Basilica is lined with salami and prosciutto panini stalls and so I imagine it would smell of meat to a dog. Arlo kept pulling me back on his lead, keen to hang around and allow the pork smells to envelop him. I was less enthused by that idea and it did seem a bit incongruous walking up to one of the world's holiest shrines and for it to smell like a transport café. Still, perhaps it's what Jesus would have wanted, what with him feeding the five thousand and all that. He does seem to have had some feel for mass catering.

St Peter's is the largest church on earth by internal area and is topped by the world's highest dome. I'm not entirely sure that when Michelangelo, Donato Bramante and Carlo Maderno set about designing it the effect they were after was a big bobble hat but I can see what Arlo means. And of course it's not a restaurant. Or indeed the mother church of Catholicism or even the cathedral of Rome. Both of these titles are held by the Archbasilica of St John Lateran about four miles away.

As you'd expect, there are thousands of onlookers and pilgrims in that piazza at all times and so there are plenty of hi-vis tabard-adorned religious stewards and indeed uniformed enforcers. There are also some undercover Vatican operatives mingling with the populace disguised as civilians.

Naturally there are a lot of nuns wandering around Rome and you can't help but notice that they are all tiny. I wonder why this is. Are short people intrinsically drawn to religious orders because a life of seclusion means they aren't struggling to be noticed when attempting to get served at crowded bars or reach stuff on high shelves at supermarkets in the outside world?

In the approach to St Peter's we encountered an impossibly minuscule old woman dressed in black robes from head to toe, which was a distance of just over a yard. She could have been a nun, or in mourning, or just someone who favoured a monochromatic wardrobe. It was hard to tell. Maybe all three. We'll never know.

She may also have been begging for money with the empty paper cup in her hand or she might have just finished her macchiato. Again, I can't be certain. However, she was unceremoniously bundled out of the way by a suave young man with pompadour quiff and trimmed stubble wearing a tight white T-shirt, undersized blazer and half-mast chinos with, as Arlo observed, no socks. This seemed quite sinister to me. Call me old-fashioned but I do like my security personnel and undercover policemen to be reassuringly scruffy and tubby. You know where you are with someone with a beer gut in a bobbled jumper with half a fried egg sandwich down it, don't you? How does the old joke go? Two scruffs waddle into a bar and the barman says:

'Hey, are you guys cops or just lousy dressers?'

Get this, though. Francis is nearly ninety now but one of the jobs he did in his earlier days in Buenos Aires was nightclub bouncer. Wow. Maybe he's personally responsible for training these heavy-handed goons who are out and about moving minute Mother Superior mimics along.

To be fair, I suppose you do need efficient policing of the papal precincts as you're bound to get the occasional obsessive oddball trying to get close to the big guy or any passing cardinal. These 'made-men' of the faith are treated like rock stars and visiting potentates, and so I did wonder if you could perhaps disguise yourself as one if you bought the right garb.

There are quite lot of ecclesiastical clothing stores in that part of town. A cassock from Mario Bianchetti Ltd was priced at €345. One of those cool wide-brimmed 'Saturn' hats to go with it came in at €175. (You can get a bishop's mitre for €250 but I think this might draw a bit too much attention to yourself.) So for €500 or so you could kit yourself out as a priest. I'd like to see those slender fashionista bully boys manhandle you then.

We did go into one of these 'Moss Bros for clerics' shops and enquired whether you needed to produce some kind of permit proving you were the real holy deal before you were allowed to buy. The ever-so cheerful lady behind the counter said that technically you didn't. She admitted that she was only really supposed to sell to the genuinely ordained but she had no way of knowing for sure. This means that you could kit yourself out as a cardinal and get total respect and genuflection everywhere you went. I bet you would get the best table and jump the queue at Tonnarello, too, so it's maybe worth thinking about.

Arlo wasn't allowed in the biggest church on the planet and so had to wait while we took turns. He seemed quite happy about it, though, because as I reported back to him it smelled a good deal less meaty inside than on the approach. Again, I think this is what Jesus would have wanted. Happy though he would be to feed the multitudes on their way to pay homage at the world's largest bobble hat, I doubt he would have approved of a hot-dog stand in the Chapel of the Blessed Sacrament.

The Local Park (Villa Sciarra)

Today was totally the best day so far. We went up some steps. Obviously. They weren't Spanish or anything. They were just steps. They really love steps here. They're mad on them. I wonder why?

Anyway, at the top of these steps was a gate and inside was some grass and paths and fountains and some small structures made out of planks and scaffolding, which must have been a building site making something for some little people, like maybe those tiny nuns or something. We have similar things at home in that town I won't remember until I smell it again.

So the good thing that made today the best was that I could get off the lead and chase after whatever it was that was rustling in the bushes. Some of these bushes were on the edge of a steep drop which gave Him and Her the willies. As if I can't see a cliff edge right in front of my face. I'm only teasing them, the gullible fools, so I'm having the last laugh.

Although not for long actually as I was back on the lead pretty soon, but I'll still have the last laugh when I go awol in the Sistine Chapel. Anyway. It was still totally the best day yet.

It really wasn't, but it does give you an insight into what the canine mind considers to be pure pleasure, and that is running off the lead in a park. The rustling in the undergrowth was due to scampering lizards. We'll return to those, but we don't get a lot of them in the town he won't remember until he smells it again. Strange sentence that, wasn't it? He doesn't remember Knutsford but he knows he will remember it when the smell reminds him that, for a while at least, he didn't remember it. Animal psychologists and behaviourists will no doubt have a lot to say about this in some scientific journals only available on subscription to brainboxes.

Most of Rome's parks are confusingly called 'villas' as they were previously the grounds and estates of privately owned mansions. The Villa Borghese is the biggest and most famous. Our local green space was Villa Sciarra, which seems to be well down the park pecking order. It originally belonged to Cardinal Antonio Barberini of the noble and well-connected (i.e. chummy with the Pope) Colonna family.

Its last private owner was George Washington Wurts, an American diplomat and art collector. His widow, Henrietta, gave it to Benito Mussolini on the condition that it was a public facility in perpetuity. Seems like quite a bit could have gone wrong with that arrangement given you're taking a Fascist dictator at his word, but accessible to all it remains. It's a bit scruffy, though, and some of the fountains don't work. That's the legacy of communism, I suppose. Look at what happened to the Spomeniks in the Balkans after Tito.

The collection of 'small structures' Arlo refers to was a kids' playground. Just as elephants and lions look small on the telly, I suppose it did look like a tiny construction site when you think about it. Probably subject to the same health-and-safety protocols and a good thing too. When I was a kid in Bolton there was a hugely tall slide in Queen's Park. Every square foot of that play area was luxuriantly topped with a bed of springy and lovingly kept turf. Except under the slide itself, a zone subjected to heavy infant footfall, where a circle of rock-hard tarmac had been laid to ensure any tumbling tot would suffer, if not compound fracture, then at least concussion.

Arlo is correct that there are a lot of steps in Rome, but then it's not flat. The presence of hills is something most people, if not dogs, know about.

Essentially, as you'll have heard, there are seven: the Capitoline, Quirinal, Viminal, Esquiline, Caelian, Aventine and Palatine. Actually, though, there are eight as our nearest hill, and the location of this park, is the Gianicolo, which is also known as the Janiculum.

To complicate matters further, there's also Vatican Hill, though as it's in a separate nation state, does it count as part of Rome at all, even though it lies at its centre? It's confusing. Officially Vatican Hill, at 75 metres, is the second highest peak after the Viminal. It doesn't look that big. I think Pope Frank's predecessors muscled in on the Roman hill scene and are just talking themselves up. That's organised religion for you.

It must be right, though, as I looked it up in a book. Mind you, just because it's in a book doesn't make it true, does it? I mean, look at the Bible. I know, I know. One person's truth is another's fairy tale. I'm also conscious of writing this under the watchful if restless gaze of my Pope Francesco bobblehead. It is of a higher quality than expected. Ed was right.

Arlo loved his outing. He was free to roam to some extent and scan the tree branches for squirrels. There weren't any but I'm not sure that really matters to him. Like a fisherman deep in contemplation waiting for a nibble, sometimes it's the anticipation that counts. On one occasion, he did get a scent and charged off at the sort of speed that's easily attainable if you've got four legs and weigh eight kilos. I assumed he had been alerted to movement in the undergrowth but it turned out he was drawn to the aroma of a discarded gelato melting on the pathway. Proving that indeed it is the hunt and not the capture that really matters, he took one desultory lick of it and then trotted on. The fussy little pampered prince.

It was a perfectly pleasant outing in the late-morning sunshine but it really wasn't anything special from a human perspective. But when you stay somewhere for quite a long time, some days are a bit boring. We also bought cleaning products.

Trevi Fountain

Today we went to a sort of big paddling pool. Funnily enough, no one was in there and I'm not surprised. Some of the water splashed on me and it was freezing. I hate water. I'll drink it when I absolutely have to because, let's face it, I'm not given much choice, am I? Why can't I have a holiday drink of choice? That orange stuff with an orange in it smells brilliant.

I was pleased to be on the move, though, as we'd spent quite lot of time in a boring shop in the morning while He tried some stupid shirts on that all looked rubbish even if She lied and said that one of them was great and so He kept it on and off we went. It was dead funny then when one of those things with flapping wings swooped down and did a poo on Him. Honestly, you couldn't make it up. Me and Her loved that.

Now, we always clear up after ourselves wherever we go, if you get my drift. But lots of disrespectful yobs were chucking stuff into this pond. Coins mainly. What a waste of money. You could use that to buy bottles of tap water at the Spanish Steps. Apparently this pool with big fancy spigots is in a famous film. We watched it on the big couch in our little house up the steps but I didn't like it because in the first part of that scene the blonde woman had a cat on her head.

Bizarrely, this is true. It happens in the classic 1960 Federico Fellini film *La Dolce Vita*. In one of cinema's iconic moments the Swedish celluloid siren Anita Ekberg, having detached said moggy from her coiffure, frolics in the waters and coaxes her co-star, Marcello Mastroianni, to join her. I don't wish to appear base here but honestly ... have you seen Anita Ekberg? You wouldn't have thought all that much coaxing was necessary. It is also said that Ekberg, being of Nordic blood, happily filmed for hours on end in the chilly flumes. The Italian Mastroianni by contrast wore a wetsuit under his clothes. Wimp.

The present Trevi design owes most to Pope Urban VIII, who, in 1629, said to our old friend Bernini Jr: 'Oi, Gian Lorenzo, this fountain needs a makeover. Could it have some big fancy spigots?'

'Your Holiness,' came the reply, 'I'm a Baroque sculptor. Big and fancy is what I do.'

The location of this landmark comes as something of a surprise. If you're expecting it to be lying in state at the far end of a wide Renaissance piazza, you'll be disappointed. You just turn a corner from a narrow shopping street and it's there, although you might have to elbow a few hundred tourists out of the way to see it. It is beyond Spanish-Steps-crowded and it doesn't feel entirely safe having that many people kettled in such a tight space. I believe they are thinking about making a nominal charge to view it to regulate the number of people there at any one time, and that seems like a sensible idea to me.

The Trevi has an interesting relationship with money. Not unreasonably, Arlo is unaware of the tradition of throwing coins rather than rubbish into its once Ekberg-inhabited lagoon.

If you're following the rules to the letter, you're supposed to chuck three separate coins with your right hand over your left shoulder with your back to the water. Obviously. If you did it the other way you'd risk taking someone's eye out.

The first coin means you will come back to Rome, the second that you'll find love and the third that you will get married in the Eternal City, so if you don't want the expense and inconvenience of getting hitched abroad then you're best sticking at two.

Here's something, though. About €1,250,000 a year goes into that fountain. That money is collected and used to fund food banks and subsidised stores for the city's poorest individuals. How great is that?

People do throw other stuff in there, of course, including medals, jewellery, ice-cream tubs, dentures and, on one occasion, an umbilical cord. Hard to work out exactly what happened there. Did someone give birth on that actual spot or, planning ahead, did they save it at the hospital and keep it in a Tupperware box until they were in front of the gushing torrents?

Perhaps people deposit all this stuff mistakenly thinking that the Trevi bestows general good luck in an ornate wishing-well style. That would explain why several misguided and gummy individuals have chucked their false teeth in, convinced of the subsequent miraculous regrowth of their missing gnashers. Presumably most of them now live on minestrone.

Talking of omens of luck, it used to be universally taken as a sign of impending good fortune if a bird defecated on you.

Oddly enough this happened to me en route to the Trevi and on my newly purchased and not inexpensive linen shirt. I was tempted to overcome my resistance to cold-water swimming and take it for a rinse in the fountain. Oh, and if you're thinking of taking a dip then be warned, it is freezing and you will get fined. Then again, your penalty payment goes on a pauper's pizza so even though you're going to get arrested and do a lot of shivering, you've still performed a charitable act. Well done you.

Arlo is right that he only drinks water and seems to exist on just a couple of noisy laps of the bowl a day. I imagine therefore that a big orange drink might look quite tempting.

He's referring to the ubiquitous Aperol spritz. I love it but it's quite a bitter drink. How has it taken over the world? Or at least those parts of it where the sun shines. It is a drink that needs sunlight as its extra ingredient. Drinking it in the Piazza del Popolo in twenty-five degrees with a cloudless sky seems entirely right. It just wouldn't be the same in a steady drizzle at Crewe bus station.

But is really has conquered Rome in a way not seen since the Visigoths.

Hadrian's Villa and a Pork Sandwich

Look there's another one! There are loads of them. What are these weird little speedy greeny-yellow things scurrying about like skinny frogs on legs? Surprise, surprise, we're hanging around by some more stones and these darting critters are everywhere.

We went out in the car today. Cars are brilliant, aren't they? You just get in, fall asleep and when the engine stops you wake up and you're there. Wherever 'there' is. It's a totally stress-free mode of transport. Look, there's another critter!

So where is 'there' today? Well, as I say, there seem to be a lot more piles of stones. I think there must have been some kind of dispute with the builders, though, because this job looks a long way off being finished. You know, like Jim and Sophie's extension next door at the home I've forgotten about. Apparently it's an 'orangery' but it seems unnecessarily big to me. How many oranges can anyone need? Even in all those drinks.

Look, there's another one. Where do they keep disappearing to? One second they're right there, the next, vanished into thin air. To be honest, I was quite glad to get out of there. I couldn't be let off the lead because someone called an emperor said so or something and he seems to make the rules around here. It was torture not being able to chase these things properly like I do with the squirrels at home. Look, there's another one! And another one! And two more! They're all over the place.

Thankfully we went back in the car and I had pork for lunch in a different place, which we got to in just a few minutes. Aren't cars brilliant? Look, there's another one.

This all happened at the Emperor Hadrian's country retreat, which is about an hour out of town heading south.

The frogs on legs Arlo refers to are lizards. Frogs are, of course, already on legs except in France, where they've eaten them all. Incidentally the many ornamental ponds at Villa Adriana were full of tadpoles so it looked like there were going to be a lot more frogs on legs hopping around there very soon.

Lizards filled the squirrel-shaped hole in Arlo's everyday existence. He loves to chase a squirrel and, as he said earlier, has special noises he saves for just those occasions. You do get squirrels in Italy but none in Rome that I've seen, despite there being lots of trees. So he focused his hunting instincts on these lightning-fast reptiles known as Italian wall or ruin lizards. If you want to get really nerdy about it: *Podarcis siculus* of the family Lacertidae. When in Rome, give something a Latin name.

He's kind of right about cars. They are brilliant at taking you where you want to go but, curled up in his fluffy car seat back there, he is blissfully unaware of the stress driving can bring.

Cruising down the motorways in Italy and France proved to be a thoroughly pleasant experience compared to the often-congested equivalents back home. French drivers are perhaps a bit more laid-back than their Italian counterparts, and often our drives resembled old postcards of British motorways from the sixties with only half-a-dozen vehicles on them. Continental autoroutes are, for the most part, only two lanes wide but in three months we never encountered one traffic jam. It really did make you feel like we lived on a small, crowded island back home.

You do have to pay tolls quite often unless you're taking the back roads but I'll take that if it means no snarl-ups.

Driving in the cities of Italy is a less calm experience. For a start, traffic lanes seem to be regarded as a vague notion rather than a hard-and-fast rule. In a way, I admire the local drivers' collective wilful disregard of being told what to do by 'the man'. All those years of dictatorial emperors have clearly left a mark. It's not an easy approach to get the hang of for the uninitiated, though. Even when I was in the right lane, which wasn't often, I was still made to feel like I was in the wrong one. Most of the cars on the road are in various states of disrepair but they all have fully functioning horns. Their drivers are also world class in gesturing. I didn't fully understand all of them but it was pretty easy to get the gist. Another stress factor is that you regularly find yourself in a queue of traffic jostling for position, all too aware that yours is the only car without a dent in it. For now.

With the Beetle still miraculously unscathed we arrived at Hadrian's Villa, or as Arlo thought of it, 'World of Lizards'. It's near a hilltop town called Tivoli and is a huge estate built around AD 120. And it is enormous. With an area of about 200 acres it's bigger than Pompeii and contains at least thirty grand buildings plus gardens, baths, temples, fountains and statues. Originally it was a kind of holiday home but Hadrian decided he liked its atmosphere more than the Palatine Hill so he decided to rule the empire from there. Accordingly, a bit like Versailles in some ways, a huge entourage of courtiers and factotums had to be accommodated, which accounts for the scale of the thing. One building alone had a hundred rooms. There's an imperial palace, although archaeologists believe Hadrian occupied a more modest suite of rooms, which included his own marble latrine. Funny, isn't it, how many of us now have bathrooms with marble features whereas back then you had to be the richest person in the world to have one? Is that a kind of progressive egalitarianism? If you weren't the emperor you had to make do in the communal latrines where you cheerfully sat alongside your peers and discussed matters of state. Think about that, MPs, when you complain about the state of the Palace of Westminster.

One of the principal attractions at Hadrian's Villa is the Golden Square. This consists of a large area surrounded by porticos and peristyles of columns in granite and marble. Now, I am of course aware that not everyone has the budget to visit this UNESCO World Heritage site, but fear not. There's another Golden Square. It's a shopping centre in Warrington, and I'm sure the effect is broadly the same. It was opened by the Queen in 1979 but, get this – it has 135 shops. The same number as the Spanish Steps. That can't be a coincidence, can it?

And talking of shops, there was no café at the villa. Just a vending machine. Arlo had a snuffle around it and seemed more interested than I would have thought, but perhaps I shouldn't have been surprised. Do you know how many times more powerful a dog's sense of smell is than ours? Take a guess. Higher. You're still way off. They can smell between 10,000 and 100,000 times more acutely than us. I felt pretty good about myself knowing I had 6 million olfactory receptors until I found out that Arlo has 300 million. But it must be a kind of torture for him when he can't get at this delightfully aromatic stuff. Even that scabby vending machine smelled great. No wonder he wanted to hang around the panini stalls at St Peter's.

Jim and Sophie's orangery is a sorry tale we don't need to go into here, but on matters of building works there is an oft-repeated adage that 'Rome wasn't built in a day'. I mean, come on, how could it have been? Hadrian's Villa took the best part of two decades to erect on its own. Of all the places to invoke in relation to a twenty-four-hour construction period, Rome would seem to be one of the least appropriate. Milton Keynes maybe. Yes, a cheap shot but at least plausible.

After strolling the extensive grounds and ruins and piles of stones at the *Podarcis siculus* Safari Park, we went to the aforementioned town of Tivoli. This should have taken just the few minutes that Arlo estimated but, due to road repairs, in fact took about an hour and a half. If that bit of 'Rome' had been built in a day it would have saved a lot of frustration.

Once we got there we did have some pork in the form of porchetta panini in a charming bottle-lined osteria, having been beckoned in by the cheerful owner and his equally welcoming wife. The sandwiches were magnificent, although we eschewed one of the proffered ingredients listed as 'lard'. We asked Signora Panini what exactly this was and she said: 'Lard, you know, fat,' while grappling her own ample midriff. We still must have looked confused and so she went away and came back with a large slab of something that, though topped with a herb crust, did look as though it was the byproduct of liposuction. The pong was awful. We politely refused. Arlo happily reclined beneath the table deigning to accept the multiple meaty morsels that came his way, and perhaps his only disappointment was the absence of lard. Imagine how that must have smelled with his multimillions of receptors. Well, even worse to me, but then I don't like fox poo either.

Oh, and if you're in Tivoli and you love fountains, then nip across the road to the Villa d'Este. They've got loads of fountains there, as demonstrated by the fact that just one of the fountains is called the Fountain of a Hundred Fountains. I didn't count them but it looked about right. That wasn't built in a day either.

The Tiber (or lack thereof)

'Me and Him and a mystery river.'

What, there's a river?

This is not as daft a question posed by Arlo as you might think, and I'm reminded of my friends Mike and Kellie, who, on learning that their daughter Fiona had professed to being underwhelmed by the Sistine Chapel, asked:

'But did you look up?'

To which the answer came:

'I don't think so. Why?'

Remarkable that when entering that hallowed space the word 'ceiling' never popped into your head, isn't it?

However, if the existence of Michelangelo's WORLD-FAMOUS cornerstone of Renaissance art came as news to Fiona, then the existence of the Tiber similarly passed Arlo by. It's more understandable though. From where he stands, you don't see it. Being unaware of it flowing for 430 km through Tuscany, Umbria and Lazio, he wouldn't be thinking about it. Not knowing that Rome was founded on its banks in 753 BC, it wouldn't occur to him to look for it. With no cognisance of the Father of the River, the god Tiberinus, saving Romulus and Remus when they were abandoned on its embankment, he wouldn't wonder where it was.

It is there though. It flows right around the city as you would expect but sits very low in stone-lined channels built between the

1870s and 1920s to prevent flooding. Well, mission accomplished, I suppose, but it does leave the river out of sight and to some degree out of mind. You only really pay attention to it as you amble across one of the many bridges and register its colour. It is sometimes called the *flavus* in Latin – 'the blonde' – due to its supposedly yellow coloration derived from clay. I say 'supposedly' because it looks more like sage green to me. Distinctive and not unattractive.

But if you come to Rome expecting something like the Seine or the Thames, or virtually any other river flowing through a city anywhere, with banks lined with al fresco bars, coffee shops, artisan markets and workshops, pop-up bookstores, bobblehead stalls and buskers, then put that notion out of your mind. There's nothing on its banks at all.

There is a Sunday bric-a-brac market at the Ponte Milvio but it's quite a way out of the centre. It will take you over an hour to walk there. Worth noting if you go that there was a battle there in AD 312 between the forces of the emperors Constantine I and Maxentius. Also worth noting that there have been several battles since between the forces of the local football teams AS Roma and SS Lazio.

But if you're anticipating the Tiber waters to be a bustling Canaletto Grand Canal-like scene of pleasure cruisers, motorboats, gin palaces, Bateaux Mouches, rowing skiffs, pedalos, kayaks, paddleboards and perhaps even the odd replica gilded galley, you're going to be sorely disappointed. There is literally no river traffic. The Romans pay it no attention at all, which is a pretty much unique situation for a major metropolis in my experience. They do have something called Tevere Expo along a stretch of embankment. This runs from June for a few weeks with pop-up stalls that promise food, drink, artisan artists and craftspeople, music, theatre and dance. And if photographs of previous years' events are to be believed, quite a lot of table football, or 'foos-ball' as they dub it. Obviously these seasons are popular or they wouldn't keep doing them but it does make you wonder why they ignore the river the rest of the time.

You can walk or cycle along it but its towpaths are fairly charmless, weed-infested, concrete-reinforced, graffiti-adorned places for the most part. You will also occasionally come across small clusters of tiny tents occupied by the homeless.

There are a couple of passenger craft puttering in a vaguely desultory fashion up and down the limited navigable parts above the weir from the only river island in Rome, the Isola Tiberina, to the Castel Sant' Angelo, but when I say a couple I mean literally that. One or two. Maybe three. It's perfectly pleasant feeling the breeze on your face as you chug upstream but you don't see much. You might also come off with a stiff neck as you're travelling so low in the channel that you have to look up all the time.

There are a few houseboats, and the odd closed-down bar where someone has had a doomed attempt at kickstarting some kind of waterside culture. This now seems to consist of one snack bar on a barge with a windmill on the top deck, and one quite swanky-looking floating restaurant, which was very busy. And that's it. There was a little aquarium but that seems to have failed, sadly. Oh, and there's some kind of fire station, from what I can make out. Well, I suppose you're never going to be short of water.

You're advised not to drink it, by the way. Why do you think the Romans built all those aqueducts bringing fresh water into the city? Yes, fair enough, they were showing off, but there were practical reasons too. It's illegal to swim in it as well. Like the Trevi Fountain. But even if Anita Ekberg was tantalisingly beckoning you in, you'd still take a raincheck.

Street Life and the
Capuchin Crypt

We've been walking a lot every day. I said it was about a thousand steps up to our new house and They seem to have copied me because They now keep talking about doing 'so many thousand steps' too. Anyway, however many thousand it is, it's a lot more for me. I'm not complaining. I like being out. Going for a walk is as good as life gets for dogs except for maybe roast lamb.

But there are quite a lot of obstacles on the streets here. Sometimes it's just so crowded that He has to pick me up. I'm quite glad about that. How would you feel being eight inches off the ground in a seething mass of people? From my perspective, human legs look like the trunks of those big trees that have something to do with horses and chestnuts where the squirrels run about at what used to be home.

Also on the pavements you get quite a lot of people sitting down and blocking the way. Some of them are just sitting there but some of them are doing some kind of painting. She does that on the kitchen table at home, which seems a much better place to do it than on the floor by the side of the road.

Earlier I was stuck by the kerb for quite a while because They took turns going into somewhere I wasn't allowed. Apparently there were loads of bones in there, which seems like exactly the kind of place a dog would want to go, so to be barred seems well tight.

After that, we went to some more piles of stones, which looked like all the other piles of stones but were evidently really important piles of stones, and it became apparent that I wasn't supposed to be there either. She said something about if we were challenged we would say I was an assistance dog. I mean, look at me. Even I could see that was a stretch.

And here's another thing. Some old dogs ride around in prams. I get that. They've done their how-ever-many-thousand-steps for years and so deserve to take it easy. Little kids ride around in prams too but whereas their pushchairs can go round the piles of stones, ours can't. How is that fair? These sprogs are young and can walk miles.

Yes, up to a point, although I did hear one little lad aged perhaps five or six plaintively exclaim: 'But Dad, I'm allergic to walking.'

The 'piles of stones' Arlo refers to are indeed very important. They are the remains of the Forum, one of the key sites of the city, and indeed Western democracy.

Looking down at Arlo as he dutifully trots along beside me, glancing up if I mention his name and check he's doing okay, I can sense that though there are towering remains and crumbling columns in evidence, it must all look a bit samey from his perspective.

But these structures are what's left of the Temple of Castor and Pollux, the Mamertine Prison and the Arch of Titus.

I have to admit we did rather sneak into this historic plot. We were walking round a small park and saw some people emerging from a turnstile. We peered through and recognised it as the Forum. Not overthinking it, we simply gently squeezed through the gate and started casually to perambulate the sacred grounds. It was only when we got to the other end and saw a queue of about five hundred people waiting patiently to get in that we realised we had avoided not only the queue by entering through one of the exits but also the price of admission. Dogs are technically allowed in there but only in a special carrier, which you have to provide yourself. I mean, who keeps one of those handy on the off-chance you want to amble around some sacred piles of stones, eh?

Sheepishly we managed to sneak out of the front gate while the security guards were dealing with an unruly party of schoolchildren in orange baseball caps.

If you're really obsessed with Roman history, then by all means queue up and pay the admission fee while installing your pooch in a bespoke basket, but, to be honest, the remains are all at a lower level than the pathways surrounding them, so you can pretty much see everything for free while your canine pal trots merrily along beside you. Admittedly you can't read all the detailed information next to the exhibits, but there are signs at street level showing you where everything is/was, and if you need more than that ... google it!

The bone depository that Arlo expressed an interest in was the sacred crypt of the Capuchin friars. It's underneath the church of Santa Maria della Concezione dei Cappuccini just off the Piazza Barberini. There you will find the skeletal remains of myriad members of that brotherhood sculpted into bizarre patterns and arrangements. There are five small ossuaries with niches and arches filled with cadaverous crosses, and curios made from all manner of human bones arranged on every surface, including the ceiling if you look up, Fiona. It is deeply strange and quite unsettling. The order maintains that it is not supposed to be macabre but a reminder of the fleeting nature of life on earth. Fair enough, but it's quite hard to cling on to that idea once you've seen the Chapel of the Pelvises.

The Capuchin order was founded in 1528 but I know what you're wondering. How are they connected to Capuchin monkeys and, more importantly, did they invent the cappuccino? Apparently the monkeys are indeed named after the light-brown robes the monks wore and there is some suggestion that the ubiquitous pale coffee nomenclature has a similar root. In fact, there are those who say that the iconic drink was invented by a Capuchin friar called Marco d'Aviano after the Battle of Vienna in 1683, where he served alongside Lorenzo Latte and Giuseppe Macchiato.

As far as the recumbent individuals obstructing the pavements go, they fall into several categories. Some are just your run-of-the-mill city beggars, who don't seem to be especially prevalent in Rome.

The ones with paper and paints are street 'artists'. I put the word 'artists' in inverted commas advisedly because they're not really artists at all. They're people who've bought some paintings to sell, pretending to be artists. Or if they are artists, it's quite a coincidence that they've all chosen to paint the Colosseum from exactly the same angle. In the same colours.

Even more oddly, they seem to have a shared admiration for the Rialto Bridge, which isn't even in Rome. They must make more than I thought from their 'art' if they can afford to commute backwards and forwards to Venice.

Look, guys, we know you haven't painted these daubs, and putting a tin of paints and some brushes in a jam jar of dirty water next to them isn't going to convince us otherwise. I suppose it might if you got off your phones and pretended to use said art supplies.

In a similar vein are the sand 'sculptors'. At first glance their creations look quite impressive, but again the subject matter is suspiciously repetitive. Sleeping cats and dogs mainly. What these charlatans do is get to their chosen pitches early and construct the artwork by filling a big jelly-mould type of thing then tipping it out. Like making a sand pie on the beach. They then spend all day with a tiny trowel minutely adjusting one leg of the cute pet so it looks like they're putting the finishing touches to their master-piece. And this in the city of Bernini! Scandalous.

There are also quite a lot of street 'entertainers', particularly around the Forum and the Colosseum. I gave €5 to a tubby bloke in a denim gilet cheerfully murdering 'Hotel California' on an Ovation acoustic guitar plugged into a really loud amplifier. It was compelling. Every single time he went for the top note, he missed it. He truly was the Les Dawson of the six-string. I stayed for all of it. And it was quite long.

Arlo sat patiently at my feet, questioning his life choices. Or cer-tainly questioning mine. He kept looking up at me with a gently tilted head and slightly furrowed brow as if to say:

Really? We're in one of the world's cultural epicentres and we're hanging about listening to this?

In a way I was quite surprised he seemed disdainful of this song strangler's struggle. He's listened to me playing the guitar and singing enough. He should have been used to it. Then again, I do usually get there in the end and it didn't seem likely that this guy was going to perfect that perennial Eagles favourite if he devoted the rest of his life to it.

I guess the concept of practising something repeatedly is alien to Arlo. That must be a great way to live, as if you can't do it you just don't bother. But if Michelangelo had thought the same way we'd have missed out on quite a lot, wouldn't we?

On the subject of street 'entertainment', you also see a good few living 'statues'. Again, I use the inverted commas advisedly because very few of these performers seem to have fully embraced the concept of standing still that is central to the notion of statuary. Someone dressed in a Tutankhamen death mask and full-length gold sheath was just nodding their head and waving at children. That's not statuary. That's fancy dress. But at least the costume was of a recognisable character. By way of contrast, a rotund fellow wearing white face paint and some sort of shiny robe was just energetically gesturing to passersby in the direction of his money tin. Again, that's not a living 'statue'. It's a pallid fat bloke shrink-wrapped in a shower curtain. He was getting nothing from me. I mean, Bernini must be rotating in his tomb. Which incidentally is in the Papal Basilica of Santa Maria Maggiore. It's a little more restrained than you might expect.

Caravaggio for Free

One of the great things about me is that I'm cheap to run. I don't really need anything. I see lots of families with kids who are dressed in clothes, which I don't need, wanting meals and ice creams buying for them, which I don't need, and whinging about walking everywhere and being 'allergic' and stuff, which I don't do. I've got a coat, which I hate, but it's warm and dry here so I don't need that. I drink out of fountains and puddles if I have to, and just wait till I get home to have some kibble with a bit of meat or fish in it. These brats are always eating those round things with red and yellow stuff on them. How much are those then? I'm thinking maybe a thousand pounds.

I'm so low-maintenance it's untrue. Having said that, I wouldn't mind some of those shades they put over their eyes when the sun comes out. I don't really need them, of course, but they do look kind of cool. I think people in Italy generally look a bit cooler than the scruffy sods back home, wherever that is. Even though they don't seem to be trying too hard. It looks like they've just chucked on whatever clothes were handy and not spent too long brushing their hair or anything. A bit like me. I never brush my hair. Sometimes it gets brushed for me but I hate that nearly as much as wearing a coat. But everyone looks kind of funky here. Especially the policemen.

Anyway, all I'm saying is that I'm a total bargain, which is just as well because you don't get anything for free here. Well,

I say that but we did hang out on some white marble steps for
quite a while today. I've no idea why but I assume that didn't
cost anything?

It didn't, but these were the steps of the Church of San Luigi
dei Francesi where we took turns to go in and look at the
Caravaggios. For free. There are three huge paintings there on
the walls of the Contarelli Chapel. There are only about eighty
known Caravaggios anywhere in the world so three buckshee is
some deal. There are others in Rome as well, in the basilicas of
Sant' Agostino and Santa Maria del Popolo. You can see them all
without paying a penny.

However, despite there being no admission charge, there are
some entry restrictions. While I was waiting on the steps with
Arlo I saw a young woman get turned away because her skirt was
too short. It was above the knee but certainly nothing indecent. I
couldn't see a problem myself but the security guard was having
none of it. I found this a bit rich as he was not only wearing a
hi-vis tabard but also hi-vis trousers, which I found much more
offensive than the skirt. Who appointed him the chief of fashion
police?

A young girl with her family approached wearing shorts. He
declined to let her in until she removed her sweatshirt and tied it
round her waist to cover her bare thighs. Or at least cover them at
the front. He made her wear it dangling down her body thereby
leaving her legs bare at the back. What was the point in that? And
is God really bothered what we're wearing? Certainly I could see
that expecting to be granted admission in budgie smugglers might
be a bridge too far, but a kid in a pair of shorts? Here's a quote
from Samuel, chapter 16, verse 7: 'People look at the outward

appearance but the Lord looks at the heart.' Seems pretty conclusive to me.

We're back to Arlo's earlier reflection on the central dichotomy of the lack of inclusivity of the 'All things bright and beautiful' scenario. Here again were some of the 'creatures great and small' being barred from God's house. Some for being dogs and some for wearing shorts. There have got to be worse religious crimes than that, surely.

Arlo slumped on the steps in a way that expressed resignation and ennui. He's good at that. He plonks his head flat on the ground and looks up as if to say:

You do what you want. I'm totally not bovvered.

Having been deemed to be not flouting any unwritten dress-code rules, we were granted access. Nothing can quite prepare you for what you are about to see. Like the vast majority of Roman churches, there are ornate and exquisite paintings and sculptures on every surface, including the ceilings, Fiona. But without wanting to disrespect the work of all the other hugely gifted artists whose work is on display there, they more or less disappear from your vision when set next to the works of Michelangelo Merisi da Caravaggio.

He was born in Milan in 1571 and died at the age of thirty-eight. He was evidently a bit of a lad and got into numerous scrapes and not a few fights in his short life. But what a life. As Bernini is to sculpture in Rome, Caravaggio is to painting. The trio of master-pieces are *The Calling of Saint Matthew*, *The Inspiration of Saint Matthew* and *The Martyrdom of Saint Matthew*. They're all truly wondrous but *The Calling* is the pick of the bunch in my view. It's a scene in a tavern where Jesus comes to summon Matthew to become one of his apostles. There is some discussion among scholars as to which of the figures seated at the table actually is the titular disciple. Some say it's the bearded figure seemingly point-ing at himself in a 'who me?' kind of way. Others maintain this individual is pointing at the younger man bending over on the far left. What's truly breathtaking, though, is the way the light comes in from an unseen source and illuminates the hand of Christ. You know, I'm not religious but you see that and wonder if there was some divine force at play. How could Caravaggio achieve what no one else could? This light and shadow effect is called 'chiaroscuro' (literally 'light/dark') and viewed in situ it will blow your mind. Or at least it should. If it doesn't then I feel sorry for you because the rest of us think we've seen something transcendental.

The chapel is actually quite gloomy but a light goes on and off so the paintings aren't illuminated all the time to help preserve their lustre for future generations. An American woman jostled me rather and said:

'Are these them?'

'The Caravaggios? Yes, these are them.'

'I can't see them properly.'

'A light will come on.'

'Does that mean I have to wait?'

I resisted stating that she was about to see some of the art wonders of the world, for free, that had been on those walls for over four centuries. Waiting another minute or two wasn't really worth making a fuss about, was it? I wished she'd come in shorts and been turned away.

The 'round things with red and yellow stuff' on them are, of course, pizzas and Arlo's guess on the price is off the mark by about £990 on average. That makes them cheaper in Rome than in most places in the UK. They're not free but there is plenty of stuff in Rome that is. It has the biggest concentration of antiq-uities anywhere in the world and it costs you nothing to walk round marvelling at the statues, fountains, buildings and ruins. It's the greatest free show on earth in many ways. And as if that's not enough, you can see some of the great masterpieces of art in the various churches, which, of course, do not charge an admission fee.

I know what you're thinking, though. This is just the sort of thing you would dread as a kid on holiday. Arlo is an ideal surrogate child as he may well be less than enthralled with what the plan for the day is but he has no way of knowing it in advance or expressing disappointment at the way it turned out. Until he flops his head down flat. Imagine how different that would be in the company of an overconfident and indulged miniature human.

'Where are we going today, Dad? Parascending? Whale watching? Rollercoaster riding? White-water rafting? Go-karting?'

'No, we're going to see some fascinating Renaissance paintings in a church.'

'You're kidding, right? Aren't vacations supposed to be more fun than being at home, not less? It's not free by any chance, is it?'

In terms of matters of style, Arlo makes a fair point. There seem to be fewer people in jogging bottoms wandering the sun-kissed streets here. I don't think any Italian would think of going out in their slippers or with their hair in curlers. They are casually stylish without looking like they've really thought too much about it. Which maybe means they have. But there is a devil-may-care rather than devil-wearing-Prada elan to a lot of the Roman populace.

I don't know why he was paying particular attention to the Carabinieri, as the military police are known, unless he was worried about breaking the rules and being off the lead in the park or sneaking into the Forum. They do look quite cool and wear grim expressions and massive machine guns.

The traffic cops take it too far, though. Yes, they have dashing knee-length black leather boots and jodhpurs with a stripe down the side. These are quite tight, however, so if said bobby is sporting a beer gut there is a kind of potato-on-a-stick effect. The thing that makes them ultimately uncool, though, is that they obviously think they look cool and there is nothing more uncool than that. They're just a bit too pleased with themselves to really carry it off. Maybe don't say that if they pull you over for running a red light.

The Mystery Tour to the Frog King Fountain of the Coppedè Quarter

Today was quite confusing. For a lot of it I had no real idea where we were going or why. It started off as normal, walking past the fruit and vegetable market with no good smells because there is no fish or meat. Rubbish.

Then it got weird. We stood still for a bit in the middle of the road until a big, creaky shed on wheels came up the street very, very slowly. Part of the wall slid open and we had to squeeze inside because it was full of people with things in their ears looking very grumpy. I was between His legs on the floor, which was dirty and smelly, but not in a good way, like when a fox leaves something behind, and so I decided to look grumpy too. When in Rome.

Anyway, we went on a very slow, creaky, grumpy ride for a bit before getting off and then getting on another big, creaky shed to take another very slow, creaky, grumpy ride back the other way. Then we got off the big, creaky shed and stood in the middle of the road for a bit longer by the side of a big gateway. Then, guess what? We got on an even slower and creakier shed on wheels before we got off that and tried to get into someone else's car. Well, nobody would let us get in their car so we got on another shed on wheels to go slowly and creakily back the way we'd been before to a big gateway. What was all that about then? It was a rotten trip out. Where were we supposed to be going?

But then, after a bit, a nice man did let us get in his car and we went and sat in a café and had a boring cabbage sandwich and then I had a drink out of a fountain.

Then everything got better because we went to a nice park and I had a good run off the lead before we got on another shed on wheels. This one was quite nice, though, and didn't creak and went quite fast. Funny old day. I was quite glad to get home, truth be told.

So was I, in a way.

Our experience of public transport here was not without its frustrations, though I would have to accept it may have been our own fault.

The 'sheds on wheels' are trams, which were, of course, full of people with earbuds in scrolling on their phones like they are the world over.

The trams in Rome are not massively useful to tourists because they don't go into the city centre really. They can't, as we've established: every time they try to extend the network and start digging they hit more remains of temples or basilicas or catacombs or something else of archaeological interest. I'm told a recent mayor was all for just ignoring what's down there and putting the transport needs first. That didn't go down terribly well. I can see the conundrum. Yes, the sites discovered are of significant interest but they've already got more of those than anywhere else in the world and they do need a city that works for the twenty-first century.

Incidentally there are no congestion or emission charges in Rome simply because, though the buses are pretty good, the trams only patrol the periphery and the underground is limited, so most people have no way of getting around other than by car. I guess there'd be uproar if you introduced congestion charges, but then there is everywhere for a while.

Environmentally, the Eternal City is odd for a visiting Brit. For a start, absolutely everything comes in a free plastic bag.

There are things that are different here that we take for granted in the UK. Most restaurants have no vegan options and no disabled access or toilets. Most of them have no toilet seats either and loo roll is seen very much as a luxury.

I honestly have no idea how you would cope here if you were a wheelchair-using vegan who enjoyed restaurants. My advice? Go somewhere else. Or at least carry a ready supply of tissues.

Our intention was to journey to a little-known though striking neighbourhood of architectural follies known as the Coppedè Quarter. However, our attempts to navigate the network did not go well initially. We started off by taking the wrong tram. This mistake could have been more easily corrected if we had at least been riding the wrong line in the right direction. We weren't. Returning to our original point of embarkation, we got on another tram, which was again not our intended one but at least headed vaguely towards our destination.

We eventually arrived at a hub at the city gate called Porta Portese. There's a big market there on a Sunday. It used to be quite a quirky affair, apparently, where you could pick up eccentric *objets d'art*. These days it's just full of mass-produced cheap clothing and household paraphernalia. Shame. There are a lot of vintage clothes piled up like jumble sales so I suppose you might find something worth having if you were prepared to rummage.

I wear quite a lot of vintage shirts myself, but only in the sense that I've owned them for thirty years.

There are also lots of new clothes made by brands you have

never heard of. Ross Kemp jeans, anyone? Do you know about this, Ross? Have you signed it off?

When Arlo talks about getting into someone else's car he's technically correct, but rather than getting involved in hitch-hiking or carjacking, we were just trying to summon a taxi on a busy dual carriageway. Unsuccessfully.

Arlo refused to sit down while we waited for a ride. He sniffed the air in a superior fashion and sneered slightly as if chastising me for where I had brought him. I felt the need to apologise to him as hanging about on kerbs as heavy traffic hurtled by is nowhere near as good as going to a park, clearly. His judgement of me may have been slightly harsh, as this wasn't what I'd intended, but I completely got where he was coming from.

So it was back to the 'sheds on wheels'. This time we went on the right tram but again in the wrong direction. We were getting the hang of it, I guess. At least we were now 50 per cent right rather than 100 per cent wrong. Progress. We still hadn't reached the Coppedè Quarter, which was by now taking on mythical status, but at least we hadn't got further away from it.

The other odd thing about the trams is that when we bought the tickets they were sold by time! We paid €1.50 for a hundred minutes and it was beginning to look like it wasn't going to be enough.

After about two and a half hours we did get to the Coppedè district but it should have taken about twenty minutes. It's near the Piazza Buenos Aires and is a cluster of deeply eccentric buildings designed by a Florentine architect called Gino Coppedè.

Originally conceived for a housing association around 1915, they combine elements of medieval, Renaissance, Art Deco and Art Nouveau stylings, and somehow manage to look harmonious, enigmatic and utterly amazing. There are several residences together known as the 'Villini delle Fate' or fairy houses because their roofs are peppered with miniature abodes that look intended for winged little folk to flit in and out of to their heart's content. There's the Palazzo del Rigno or 'spider building' down there, too, with its arachnid flourishes. In a way, it's all a bit Portmeirion, where Clough Williams-Ellis also let his stylistic imagination run amok to delightful effect.

You might also be moderately interested to know that a chap called Richard Harding Watt went all Italianate in parts of Knutsford. If you've ever seen the Steven Spielberg film *Empire of the Sun*, the exteriors of scenes set in the leafy ex-pat suburbs of Shanghai were actually filmed on Legh Road. If you were thinking of going to Shanghai but don't have the cash, then it's a much cheaper alternative.

We stopped for a crushingly bland sandwich of mystery filling as befitted our inadvertent mystery tour. It looked like cheese from a distance. On closer inspection it wasn't. Cabbage? As good a guess as anything. It didn't taste of much. It didn't matter. We were desperate by then.

It was all worth it, though, to see not only the idiosyncratic properties but also the elaborate spigot Arlo reluctantly drank from. This was the Frog King Fountain, which is in the heart of this eccentric locale. It does boast a lot of frogs, so no argument there, but it's also famous because the fully clothed Beatles took a splash in it in 1965.

On 27 and 28 June, they played their only gigs in Rome at the Teatro Adriano on Piazza Cavour in the part of the city called Prati. Noël Coward turned up on the second night apparently. The venue is still there and is a cinema now. After one of the shows the band went to the nearby Piper Club, and that's still there too. It gets mixed reviews with many people saying it's too crowded, which funnily enough was exactly the same experience the Fab Four had, choosing instead to frolic like four Scouse Anita Ekbergs in the cascading fountain nearby.

Paul McCartney later had a hit with the Frog Chorus. Coincidence? Yes.

The return journey was a lot less eventful once we discovered the relative simplicity of the buses. Absolutely first-rate service.

Oh, and the park we went to contained another glorious quirk of Roman architecture in the Arts and Crafts-styled Owl House. If it's your kind of thing, there's a big collection of Art Nouveau glassware in there which they refer to as 'Liberty'. Try selling that one to your kids.

'You're kidding, right, Dad? And it's not even free? Wow.'

The Open Road

There are some nice people here who let you get in their car and go for a ride to wherever you want if you don't fancy walking somewhere. How kind is that?

Today we went in a lady's car along a very straight road. I went to sleep for most of it and just woke up when we stopped. Aren't cars brilliant?

When we got out on the straight road we walked down it for a very long time. I think we walked the whole road actually. It was great because there weren't any cars or many people but there were still some piles of stones, which They love always.

This road also seemed to be made out of old stones so it wasn't very comfortable to walk on. I was beginning to wonder why I didn't have any of those gloves for feet that They wear.

Anyway, the day got even better when we went to a big green place with lots of grass and trees and big dishes to drink out of if you're a common local dog. I prefer to wait for my private supply, thanks very much.

There were lots of pale people standing pretty still but I couldn't help noticing that most of them had taken their heads off. I didn't know they could do that. Even more weird was when we went round the corner and stood by some railings for a long time and just near there were a load more still people who didn't have any bodies. Just heads! Bonkers.

Arlo is, of course, unaware that taking a taxi involves a financial transaction. What a blissful way to live. I'm so coming back as a cute dog with a nice owner, while being perfectly well aware that this rather contradicts my earlier comments about reincarnation.

The 'straight road' in question was the Via Appia Antica, or Appian Way if you prefer. We didn't walk the whole of it as that would have taken a lot longer given that it runs for 360 miles all the way to Brindisi on the Adriatic coast.

There are remnants of buildings and statues along the sections approaching Rome but after a while you start to take these things a bit for granted. There is Roman stuff everywhere and so unless it's of particular note you tend to just stroll by without taking too much notice. Some of this Roman stuff would be the absolute focus of historical sites in any other city in the world but here … it's just more stuff. You've got all the big stuff to see so the small stuff you just sort of glance at. Perhaps the more visceral experience is thinking about the striations in the cobbles you are walking on. These were made by chariots passing along the road just after its construction in 312 BC. That's quite a thought, isn't it?

As Arlo says, this doesn't provide the smoothest surface to walk on even if you have got sturdily soled 'gloves for feet'. I'm quite surprised shoes for pups aren't more of a thing really. I did wonder on the hottest days whether he might like a double pair of canine desert boots. Or perhaps he'd be interested in the DogClog™, which I'm perfecting and hoping will sweep the world like the ugliest shoe ever invented: the Croc. You can, of course, still purchase human footwear made by the classic Hush Puppies brand but they've never branched into mules for mutts. Missing a trick, I'd say.

There were twenty-nine of these ancient routes leading out of Rome to ferry supplies, services and, perhaps most importantly, armies heading out on their next deployment. Naturally you could come back the same way, leading to the famous statement 'all roads lead to Rome'. Which is clearly not right in the literal sense but also something of a truism. For the sake of argument, let's accept that these twenty-nine highways constituted 'all roads'. You would naturally assume that if they led out they must also lead back unless some very early experiments in bypasses and ring roads were being conducted. Which they weren't, as far as I can tell. Having said that, the Roman God of Returning was called Rediculus, so you never know.

Once you get beyond the San Calisto and San Sebastiano catacombs two or three miles out from the centre, the Appian Way offers a beautifully peaceful and contemplative walk or bike ride. You can also visit said networks of vaults, of which there are around sixty or so in Rome, of which seven are open to the public. I went into the ones at San Sebastiano and they are certainly atmospheric. You wouldn't want to get lost down there. It's a maze of creepy tunnels lined with burial niches as interment of bodies wasn't allowed within the city walls.

There were no bones, though, which was a bit of a swizz. Or perhaps I'd been spoiled by the Capuchin crypt and still had a head full of pelvises.

Incidentally, I learned from the guide that Saint Sebastian was persecuted for his Christianity by the Emperor Diocletian, after which 'he died completely'. That sounds drastic but on reflection I hope when I die I do it 'completely' as dying 'partially' would be much worse.

Oh, and as we've already discovered, Bernini's last work, the *Salvator Mundi*, completed when he was eighty, is in the basilica there. What a grafter he was, choosing to work till that late in life. Or perhaps the age at which his pension kicked in just kept going up.

The big dog dishes in question were drinking fountains, which, in truth, Arlo never really got the hang of. Out of complete desperation and necessity he did have a half-hearted lap at the Coppedè Quarter under the watchful eye of those frogs who'd met the Fab Four but, generally, like the finicky fellow he is, he prefers to wait until we offer him his personal bowl.

These potential hydration stations were in the largest landscaped park in the city: Villa Doria Pamphili. It's named after the Pamphili family, one of whom became Pope Innocent X in 1644. And it wasn't Mrs Pamphili. When that line died out, the villa got passed on in the eighteenth century to Prince Giovanni Andrea IV Doria, who stuck his name in there too. I guess these large 'villas' are rather like the country estates we have in the UK. They should all be public parks, shouldn't they? Just because one of your distant ancestors emptied Henry VIII's chamber pot doesn't mean you should own half of Derbyshire. For ever. If you start a business and make loads of money, fair enough – buy what you like as long as it's not the countryside or coastline we all want to share. But hereditary ownership of land is theft from the rest of us. Okay. See you on Kinder Scout.

Arlo refers to 'people standing pretty still', therefore making a stark contrast to the living 'statues' we'd seen. He didn't quite grasp the concept of statuary but he was right about the bonces. The vast majority had been lost down the years. I guess the neck is always going to be the weak spot. If only the Romans had had the foresight to invent the polo-neck jumper then the connection between the head and shoulders could have been much sturdier. There is some suggestion that the detachable nature of the noggins was intentional so that if someone immortalised in marble fell out of favour, which, let's be frank, wasn't unusual in ancient Rome, you could just whip their head off and stick a new one on without needing to re-carve the whole body. This makes perfect sense and is widely accepted to be the inspiration for Barbara Euphan Todd's *Worzel Gummidge*.

The disembodied heads Arlo mused about were busts of Italian patriots involved in the nineteenth-century unification called the Risorgimento (which means 'Resurgence'). I hadn't heard of any of them, though there are a few Garibaldis in there, so I'll just mention Giacomo Pagliari as he had the best hat.

These patriotic busts are on the Gianicolo Hill and standing there you get arguably the best panorama of the whole city. So much so that it is often dubbed 'Rome's Balcony'. If you're up there at midday, though, be warned. A single, deafening cannon shot is fired, and if you're not expecting it you might well splutter on the arancini ball you've just purchased from one of the little caravans. I knew it was coming but there was no way of warning Arlo, who literally leapt vertically with all four paws off the ground when the detonation happened. I felt guilty at not having prepared him for it, or at least equipped him with pooch plimsolls to ensure a softer landing.

This location is actually quite a distance from the Villa Doria Pamphili but I have no recollection of the journey between the two.

Perhaps I was sleeping in someone else's car.

Aren't cars brilliant?

St Peter's Knee

St Peter's Knees

'Me. Peeping out bottom right. Where's He gone then?'

Every day is a surprise to me because when we set out I've no idea where we're going. Today I thought I heard something about going to see some knees but then I thought I must have misheard that because why would anyone push through all the crowds by the biggest pile of stones to get to some knees? That makes no sense at all.

We went up the inevitable steps and there was a massive man sitting very still on a very still big horse. I then had to have my picture taken in front of a weird little statue of three creatures because one of them was a relative of mine or something. It seemed to be two mini-humans and a sort of slouching, pathetic-looking canine-type thing that didn't look like it could take on a fly let alone a postman or a swan. I don't know. If you want a noble, fearsome-looking dog to be on top of a pillar for everyone to look at then there are loads of better ones to choose from. I'm a modest soul so it's not for me to suggest myself but I'd look amazing up there.

We then went past two more men who weren't moving much, although one of them was blinking all the time, before we found this place where I'm sure They said something about knees again. I had to stay outside. Big deal. Who cares about knees? I see thousands every day at very close quarters, and once you've seen one pair, you've seen them all.

We were back by the Forum, where street artists proliferate, and yet again there was another example of failed living statuary. He was in a silver suit with a silver top hat and what looked like a silver banana in his hand. He also had a silver face so some effort had gone into the get-up but Arlo was right. He was blinking all the time. Occasionally, you can forgive, but not continuously. Perhaps he was suffering from blepharospasm, which causes rapid muscular fluctuations of the eyelid. If so, I sympathise, but if that is the case then take a really long, hard look at yourself, in one of the brief moments when your eyes are fully open, and ask if being a living statue is the career for you. If you don't suffer from that affliction, then pack it in anyway as you're obviously just not cut out for it.

Much more satisfyingly stationary was the actual statue of Julius Caesar himself, opposite the piles of stones that are what's left of his eponymous Forum. A great many people were having their picture taken with him, which seems entirely reasonable. If you think of Rome, he's probably the first name you come up with. Unless you're at the Cat Colony.

In his honour we went for lunch at Pizza Forum, where I had the Caesar salad. I know you will have been expecting a cheap Caesar salad gag for some time now, so sorry to disappoint you but I don't really have one. As you probably know, this ubiquitous dish has nothing to do with him anyway. Legend has it that it was invented in the 1920s by an Italian chef in Tijuana, Mexico, by the name of Caesar Cardini. I've no reason to doubt that but when you're in the Eternal City it's hard not to assume some association with the man some called the Greatest Roman of them all. I wonder how he would feel about the salad taking his name in the city he once ruled before coming a cropper at the cattery. I can't help feeling that the whole thing is a bit disrespectful somehow, but it was perhaps the best Caesar salad I've ever had. At Pizza Forum, you'd hope so, wouldn't you?

The huge statue of a big bloke on a massive horse is Marcus Aurelius, although it's a replica. The real one is inside the nearby Capitoline Museum so if you want to see that you'll have to pay to go in. No one will know the difference from the pic on your phone though.

The statue is at the centre of the piazza at the top of the Capitoline Hill where the Temple of Jupiter Optimus Maximus was dedicated in 509 BC. It's not there now but the site represents the absolute geographical and spiritual centre of the Roman Empire.

The photo opportunity Arlo speaks of was at the statue of a DNA-sharing, distant lupine relation of his called Lupa suckling Romulus and Remus. Given that this represents the birth of Rome and how it got its name, it's less than impressive. Marcus Aurelius looks truly heroic and monolithic but these two little whelps and the meagre she-wolf look quite apologetic.

As I held Arlo aloft to have his picture taken he turned to glance at the underwhelming figurines and stiffened slightly. He seemed to be striking quite a noble pose, perhaps aware in some subliminal way that he cut a far more imposing figure than the remote forebear without whom the Eternal City might well not have existed.

You're probably thinking that Arlo's assumption that we were trooping halfway across the city to see some knees is based on a misunderstanding. It isn't. Bear with me on this one.

Around the corner from the Colosseum, through the interminable queues seeking entry, you will find an oasis of blissful calm in the Basilica of Santa Francesca Romana, if you know where to look. It is a truly beautiful space where they play wonderful sacred music all the time to add extra atmosphere. Oddly, given the tranquillity of the place, Francesca Romana is the patron saint of car drivers and so causes gridlock every 9 March when motorists park their vehicles in the vicinity to receive her blessing. Well, I suppose some kind of sense of peace and reflection must descend on the area once everyone's well and truly boxed in.

Up some steps on the right-hand side of the altar are two indentations under iron grates halfway up the wall. These are said to be the knee imprints of Saint Peter when he was praying to the Almighty to help him discredit the magician Simon Magus, who had, rather like an early incarnation of David Blaine or Dynamo, levitated himself above the Forum to demonstrate his superiority over God and his earthly representatives. Evidently Peter's message got through, and frankly if he can't get through then who can, and the heretic sorcerer immediately fell down and died. Heaven 1 – Magic 0. Great, the forces of good prevailed, though this still doesn't explain to me how Peter's kneeling position is halfway up the wall. Was he levitating too?

To make it even more confusing there are some who say these are the patella prints not of St Peter but of St Paul.

You know, I'm beginning to wonder if some of this was made up.

A Power Station

If you get your lead on and head out of the crowded city centre, Rome has some really lovely country walks. We went on one today. There were no cars, just a few people on those funny little two-wheeled cars with no roof where their legs move up and down. I don't like those. They quite often get in my way and the people driving them seem to think they can go where they want.

Apart from that, we walked near the river and there was sweet-smelling grass as far as the nose could sniff. We crossed over a metal bridge after a bit and walked to the kind of big building that I assumed I wouldn't be allowed in as I've discovered there is a conspiracy against dogs being allowed inside big houses et cetera. To use a bit of the old Latin lingo.

Well guess what? When we went to the front door there was nobody there at all so we just strolled on in. Inside were some big lumps of metal, which made quite a nice change from big heaps of rubble, although there were still stones made to look like bits of arms and legs that used to be attached to people but had now fallen off.

After a while a woman wearing a cross face and a big badge said something in a nasty voice about dogs having to be picked up. I was quite glad about that because it had taken us hours to walk there as somebody had taken us the wrong way after misreading the map. Whose fault was that then?

It would be indelicate to say. But it wasn't Arlo's. Or mine.

The two-wheeled cars without roofs are, of course, bikes, the riders of which do seem to have a universal sense of entitlement, although in Rome everybody in every vehicle goes where they like so I suppose it's unfair to pick on cyclists.

Looking down at Arlo as he gleefully nuzzled the shrubbery, I could see that from his vantage point of eight inches off the ground he must have been secure in the knowledge that he was indeed in a bucolic idyll.

By way of contrast, the human eyeline gave you an uninterrupted vista over the lustrous verges towards the atrophied semi-derelict industrial zone of Testaccio.

As unlikely as it sounds, this was our intended destination.

We were headed for the Centrale Montemartini, which is a disused power station but with its machinery largely intact. The two gargantuan diesel engines were installed in the 1930s and were intended to help supply the planned World's Fair of 1942. The war put paid to that. How well it would have worked is open to question in any case as the engines could only be run for four hours at a time before they had to be switched off and serviced.

I had an Austin Mini Metro like that once.

In 1997, extensive renovations were taking place at the Capitoline Museum, which meant that a lot of its exhibits had to be temporarily removed and stored elsewhere. That's how quite a lot of them ended up at this mothballed plant. The original plan was to move them all back once the refurbishment was complete but people became so entranced by the Centrale's juxtaposition of antiquities and generators that it became a permanent display. And it is compelling. Originally they called the exhibition *The*

Machines and the Gods, and the brute force and sheer heft of the engineering coupled with the monumental nature of the classical statuary completely works.

There are also some really nifty mosaics to see and everything is handily signed in both Italian and English, which is how I can tell you with total confidence that the toga-wearing statue from the Barberini collection is known as 'the Barberini toga-wearing statue'. You're welcome.

It's well worth a visit even if it's a lengthy walk out of town.

You are supposed to buy a ticket, which we were more than willing to do. However, there was not only an absence of any security guard but also no one manning the ticket desk. There was literally no way of paying or checking canine access. So we just wandered through the turnstile in a nonchalant back-gate-of-the-Forum kind of way. (On a separate occasion, we also pulled a semi-inadvertent two-for-one scam at the Galleria d'Arte Moderna involving access from the al fresco coffee shop.)

After a while, an officious woman did accost us and in unnecessarily forceful terms inform us that Arlo had to be carried. As we'd had a considerable trek to get there he was perfectly amenable to this plan, and his elevated vantage point seemed to result in a greater interaction with the exhibits, over which he cast an appraising eye and investigative snuffle. Certainly his use of a *fragmentum* of Latin would seem to indicate some measure of engagement, though it's possible I'm overthinking this.

Testaccio is an area on the up. Like many inner-city zones stripped of their previous industry, it is now re-emerging as a hip and relatively affordable place to live. You can even get poke bowls there so vegan survival in Rome might be a possibility after all.

It's also home to the Corviale, which is a block of flats over a kilometre in length. It was designed in 1972 as a kind of brutalist self-contained city with thousands of residential spaces and areas for independent traders and creative types. Like all grand designs of this nature, it more or less immediately became a no-go zone for the forces of law, and though it represented an alternative way of living, it wasn't one people except the most desperate of squatters fancied adopting. If they can get that place sorted, it will really be Testaccio's crowning achievement. I assume it's dog friendly. I don't imagine that, for years, you'd have fancied going in there without one. And a much bigger and more threatening-looking one than Arlo. Which is most dogs, to be honest.

Food

'Me and Him doing nothing. (We did that quite a lot).'

They seem to talk quite a lot about food. From what I can make out, She is very interested in it and He's not.

I'm with Him. I'm not really all that fussed about eating. I seem to be able to live on fresh air and I'm wondering whether my relationship with food is a bit weird. If we go away for a couple of days, I can quite easily decide not to eat until I get back home again no matter what they tempt me with, although the bits I got of those lardy pork baps were pretty good.

I've also been getting a bit more continental in my mealtimes. Sometimes I don't have my lunch until about midnight.

The food they have here seems mainly to consist of the £1,000 round things with yellow and red stuff on and some rubbery stuff which might be called pasty or pastry or pesto or pasta or something. It comes in lots of different shapes but is basically just rubbery stuff. It is really nice, but it all tastes a bit the same.

There seem to be quite few people around here who've got some teeth missing. I'm not surprised. They don't really need teeth because none of them seem to eat anything that needs chewing. My teeth are great. I can grind a yak bar for hours on end and it is really satisfying and not remotely annoying.

Sometimes we go out and buy food. There's the unsmelly fruit and vegetable market at the bottom of our street every day. I never eat fruit or vegetables but it looks colourful even with my restricted eyesight and I quite fancy one of those big spiky things they seem so keen on here.

The other thing that's different to back wherever home is, is that I'm allowed in the supermarket as long as He picks me up. Brilliant. I can see what's on the top shelves that way, although it seems to be mainly rubbery stuff.

It really does seem like I can get in pretty much anywhere except some of those big houses where all the humans only ever seem to talk in whispers for some reason – unless we manage to sneak in when the people at the front door aren't looking. We might get told off after a bit but it still feels like a victory for dogs every time we pull it off. I think it's what's known as 'sticking it to the man'.

Right on!

Arlo's observations are fairly accurate. Bella is very interested in cuisine and will research restaurants, make reservations and take photographs of what arrives on the plate.

I will eat more or less anything if I am hungry.

Except olives, beetroot and the curse that is balsamic vinegar.

Arlo's own diet is relatively limited so it's easy to see why he might fancy one of the 'big spiky things' just for a change. These are artichokes. They love them here. I have no idea why. You can have them Romanesque style, which means sloppy and horrible, or deep-fried, which is crunchy and horrible. People say they are an acquired taste but why acquire a taste for something that is horrible? I did buy one with the intention of cooking it later and offered Arlo a scale from its outer layer. He flexed his nostrils over it for a few seconds before haughtily turning away. I haughtily turned away from it for several days myself until I eventually haughtily tossed it in the bin. Try it if you like, but bear in mind it is technically a thistle and how many of those would you scoff on a regular basis except during times of famine?

Similarly avoid the inexplicably popular drink limoncello unless the alternative is dehydration.

Oh, and he never had his lunch at midnight but he doesn't have a massively deep understanding of time.

He did sometimes manage to inhale the odd tube of penne but generally only if it had been covered in a meaty ragu. Fish he's usually happy to gobble down, but he didn't think much of pizza. He doesn't really do carbs. Perhaps that's how he keeps so trim. Dogs are smart like that. The Atkins Diet is their default setting.

Arlo's appraisal of the limited variety of dishes available is contentious but there is some truth in it. There are, as we've estimated, something like 15,000 restaurants in Rome. Based on nothing but guesswork backed up with field research in Trastevere, I would say that the menus would be interchangeable in about 14,900 of those. Don't get me wrong, the food is great and cheap and filling and freshly prepared and satisfying in every establishment, but it is broadly all the same. You get pizza (the £1,000 round things) and pasta (the rubbery stuff) obviously. You can get steak and seafood and saltimbocca (veal) and also, for some reason, tripe. They do have a deeply perverse addiction to stomach lining here. Often served with a side of thistle and a pint of limoncello. Yum.

Like Arlo and his basic contentment eating corned beef on a daily basis, I'm really not averse to a repetitive diet. There was a period of my life when, living alone, I had cheesy beans every day for lunch for three years. I haven't entirely ruled out doing it again. There is no better lunch. But the Italians are strange. It's almost as if having invented the pizza and pasta they decided that was food covered and they could concentrate on other things. Like fine art, high fashion and crashing cars.

I am probably being a bit unfair and there's no doubt you can find any cuisine you desire in Rome if you search it out. But you do have to look pretty hard. Get this, my favourite cuisine is Indian. In Italy there are around 450 Indian restaurants. Do you know how many there are in the UK? About 8,000. Let me put it another way. The most Indian eateries per capita in the UK are in Leicester. For every 100,000 people in that city there are 47 Indian food outlets. For every 100,000 people in Italy, there is 1. That's kind of incredible, isn't it? I think ultimately you have to admire their satisfaction with their delicious if limited local fare but it does have an odd effect on you. I eschew fast food for the most part but in Rome you can suddenly see a branch of McDonald's and think: *Hmm . . . something different.*

While riding in someone else's car, a very jolly cabbie asked me if we were enjoying the local eateries as the city boasted what he proudly described as 'the best food in the world'.

Mate, I thought, *have you been to the world?*

So keen are the Italians on pasta that in Trastevere there is an establishment called Laboratorio Pasta all'Uovo Il Tortellino. Literally an egg pasta laboratory in which the guys work all day every day dressed, and I swear to you I'm not making this up, in white lab coats. It's as if they're searching for the top quark or splitting atoms rather than preparing ravioli but you can't say they don't take it seriously.

There's also a restaurant here that spells out on its awning 'Qui i Famosi Rigatoni Democratici', which translates, I think, as 'Here is the Legendary Democratic Republic of Rigatoni'. So legendary is it that they don't seem to bother opening much. Its reputation and fame are that secure.

The pizza is said to originate in the south, where it was created in honour of King Umberto I's wife Margherita of Savoy. Perhaps it should have had cabbage on it (like our Frog Fountain sandwich) as well as the requisite tomato, mozzarella and basil. Incidentally, Umberto and Margherita were cousins. That's the royals for you. All this happened in Naples, talking of which ...

The Home of Pizza

Today we were in the car again. For quite a long time. I would say we were driving for about fifteen minutes. When we got there we were in what I presume was a really interesting part of town because all the buildings looked really old and knackered. They weren't quite 'piles of stones' but it looked like it was only a matter of time.

Anyway, we got out of our car and into someone else's car and drove to this big, noisy, crowded place that was absolutely awful. There was literally nothing there and nowhere I could be let off the lead. I hate it there always. Why were we even there?

Sometimes I despair of humans, even my own. We spent absolutely ages on a totally stupid street full of totally stupid shops selling totally stupid dolls and puppets. There was even one massive stupid puppet with a stupid pointy hat on and a golden nose you had to rub for good luck or something.

Having said that, things did look up a bit after rubbing the daft thing's conk as I got a well tasty bit of sfogliatella and a bit later we had some of the £1,000 round things with yellow and red on top for our tea. I then had my own bed in the hotel because we had booked something called a 'family room'. Possibly by mistake, I think. So we had a comfortable and peaceful night once I'd seen off that totally stupid cat.

That cat was indeed a genuine feline psychopath but let's set the scene for the battle.

I stress that this was Arlo's assessment and not mine but the 'absolutely awful' place was Naples. The journey from Rome was slightly longer than the slumbering pup's estimate. Fifteen minutes? Close. About three and a half hours.

As a city it is a very different proposition to the capital.

I'd be tempted to call it the Wild West if it wasn't the Deep South.

We'd elected to stay on the outskirts of the city in a district labelled the 'industrial zone', although 'war zone' would have been more accurate.

We'd booked a budget establishment that offered free parking and was dog friendly, so that clearly ruled out anywhere nice. I won't name the hotel because actually, though basic, it did a perfectly reasonable job. But it wasn't a part of town that offered much. Or indeed anything at all. Opposite was the abandoned shell of a once quite grand modern tower-block hotel called the Tiberia Palace. Its primary function currently appeared to be as a meeting place for enthusiastic vandals with a particular penchant for window smashing.

The city of Naples itself is an extraordinary assault on the senses. I felt the need to constantly check on Arlo as he negotiated at calf level a scenario that could easily have been played out on a canvas by Hieronymus Bosch, although that comparison probably wouldn't have occurred to him as he had enough on his mind appreciating Baroque sculpture without delving into the early Netherlandish school. Often I carried him as it otherwise seemed only a matter of time before he got a foot in the furry face. I could see why he might not be enjoying it much.

The general hubbub is like an overpopulated seaport crossed

with a large Spanish quarter, a Rajasthani market and the biggest Moroccan souk imaginable. The streets are narrow and teeming with life. Pavement bars and restaurants compete for space with leather-goods stalls, fishmongers performing live filleting, a smattering of grand churches, and tiny houses opening directly on to the pavements offering glimpses of the basic accommodation within. You must really have to be immune to noise to sleep at all there.

Especially if you live next door to Antonio Borelli. Antonio sings with backing tracks at deafening volume from his apartment's balcony just off the main drag. You can hear him for several hundred yards before you see him in his portly splendour giving it full bel canto from his minuscule first-floor terrace, from which hangs a basket on a rope in which you can deposit your tips. We had €5 worth.

Due to a 'no dogs' rule we decided to forgo the city's crypt, despite a tantalising sign that boasted: 'descend to the ancient cemetery and behold the skull with ears'. Naples, it seemed to me, was very much a skull-with-ears kind of town.

Arlo correctly identifies a peculiar fascination with puppets, which has a basis in local folklore. It hinges on the character of Pulcinella, who is a big deal here.

He's a kind of black-masked Mr Punch and is one of the stock characters in the Italian theatrical tradition of *commedia dell'arte* along with Harlequin, Colombina, Scaramouche, Pantalone and Pierrot among others. I've tried to watch it but I didn't find it funny. Maybe it's because I don't speak the language. I've tried to watch *Mrs Brown's Boys* too. Evidently I don't speak that language either.

There are numerous opportunities to buy a Pulcinella figure on the Via San Gregorio Armeno, also known as 'Stupid Puppet Street', but only if you are Arlo.

Naples has a huge tradition of nativity crib making but the trade has expanded to all seasons and all manner of figures. At countless shops you can buy all sorts of village and countryside scenes, clockwork artisan workers making pizzas, chopping wood or hacking at meat, and a dizzying array of character figures. These were not always easy to recognise but perhaps some were famous Neapolitans you might know if you were a native. I did identify Freddie Mercury, the Pope, Elvis, the late Queen Elizabeth II, the Joker, Elton John, Marilyn Monroe, Luciano Pavarotti, Laurel and Hardy, Karl Lagerfeld, Angela Merkel and a naked Prince Harry. (Still a prince at time of going to press, I think, but who knows? Or indeed cares?)

There were also other hideous trolls that were harder to identify with the same degree of certainty. A possible Silvio Berlusconi could equally have been Del Boy Trotter. Assuming it was unlikely there was much demand for figurines of Alf Garnett it was perhaps safe to settle on Stanley Tucci for another. One I initially took to be Susan Boyle was in fact Diego Maradona. Or Saint Diego.

They absolutely love, venerate and adore the barrel-chested 'hand-of-God' scamp here. His image is everywhere. There are murals, banners, photographs, posters, flags, replica shirts and even Diego socks. This is because his time here constitutes a modern folk tale. Pulcinella comes from the lowest tier of society but makes good thanks to his streetwise wit and guile. Diego Maradona provided a real-life parallel.

He arrived at Napoli after a then world-record transfer fee of £6.9 million from Barcelona in 1984. Seventy-five thousand fans greeted him when he was presented to the crowd on 5 July. This wasn't for a match, you understand, but just to catch a glimpse of the pint-sized cheating wizard.

The previous season the team had narrowly avoided relegation from Serie A. Under Maradona's captaincy they won the Serie A title for the first time ever in the 1986–7 season, and again in 1989–90, breaking the dominance of the northern powerhouses of Inter, AC Milan, AS Roma and Juventus. But it was more than just football. It was the south, crippled by underinvestment and home to rampant deprivation, thumbing their noses at the entitled north. Coming from incredibly poor beginnings in his native Argentina, Maradona, like Pulcinella, proved that with enough desire, belief, cunning and bending of the rules, anything was possible.

No wonder they loved him. And love him still.

There's a giant mural of him on a block of flats. When one of the complex's residents, who lives high up in the building, opens his bathroom window he appears to be living inside Diego's head.

Naples, it seemed to me, was very much an inside-Maradona's-head kind of town.

We did indeed have pizzas too. When in Rome. They were actually about a fiver and terrific. Just like they are everywhere else. I suppose that's not Napoli's fault. They invented it and everybody else has just copied it really faithfully.

Arlo slurped half-heartedly at some of the mozzarella but was clearly saving himself for the other local delicacy, called sfogliatella.

This is a sweet pastry clam shell. There are various fillings but the classic consists of a mixture of semolina, ricotta, eggs, sugar, cinnamon and citrus zest. Though it contains absolutely no artichoke or tripe it still sounds faintly disgusting, but it isn't. It's absolutely delicious.

Replete, we then returned to our accommodation, which was when we encountered one of Napoli's gangland cats. This mangy mouser had a particular swagger and a distinctly cocky look in its eye. Nevertheless we assumed it would do what felines usually do, which is to arch its back, hiss and sprint away.

Not so. Snarling, whining and with bared teeth and talons it came right at us. I snatched Arlo into my arms and directed a kick at the vicious thing to scare it off. (Don't worry, cat lovers, I didn't connect.) Arlo did get a scratch off this truculent tortoiseshell tom and let out what I'd have to admit was a slightly pathetic whimper. Still, I have to congratulate him on his refusal to engage in street fighting.

We mentioned it to the helpful woman on reception, who said that it was indeed the hotel kitty, who was 'very territorial'. Okay, but for a hotel whose only boasts are being dog friendly and providing free parking, having a resident cat that routinely attacks canine guests seems to remove one of those selling points.

The free parking?

Absolutely no complaints there.

Once you got the barrier up.

It was broken.

Most things in that area were.

Dogs and the Kingdom of Italy

'Me having a stand-off with a scooter.'

I've been here for a while now and it's pretty much fine. Well, I say 'a while' although I'm not sure I've ever lived anywhere else. Or what 'a while' is.

There are a couple of things I don't like though.

The first is broken glass. It's everywhere and as I don't wear foot gloves I feel like I'm constantly on an obstacle course. Where does it all come from?

I'm also not keen on the horrid hounds round here. At the home I've forgotten about in another country, most dogs are dead friendly like me. They trot up, give you a friendly sniff, have a little run about and then they're off with their pet human. Except for those nasty big ones owned by human idiots with tattoos and their hats on backwards. You can't trust anyone with their hat on back to front. They're not thinking straight. They wouldn't wear their trousers back to front, would they?

But most of the pooches here are quite grumpy. I don't know why. Maybe they're cross because they never get to eat any meat or chew on tough bones because they live on the same rubbery stuff as the humans. I think I'd be quite cross about that, too. Anyway, we're giving the local dogs a wide berth now. It's their loss because I'm great.

Today we queued up for ages to get into someone else's house. We did eventually get inside, and you know some people like humans to take their shoes off when they come in their house? Well, these people didn't even want me to walk on their floors. I mean, fussy or what?

After that, we went into a small tunnel for our lunch but after standing inside for a while we came out again without eating or drinking anything and went into another little tunnel down the road. That was all a bit weird. I have to say it was in a really nice part of town, though, and the dogs were much friendlier there. I think they were more chilled because they weren't surrounded by crowds all the time.

But I was still a bit confused because I never got to meet the beagles I heard them talking about.

The Beatles. Not the beagles. The Beatles. This was in Prati, where, as we've discussed, the Beatles played their only gigs in Rome at Teatro Adriano in June 1965, opposite the monumental Palace of Justice on Piazza Cavour. As we know, that's where Noël Coward came to see them and, having visited Prati, it seems like just the kind of place he would have hung out. It is an elegant and relatively sedate neighbourhood in contrast to the bustle of Trastevere. Here the buildings are late nineteenth and early twentieth century. The boulevards are wider, the graffiti less evident.

It was fully established in 1921 as the intended central administrative location for the Kingdom of Italy, which existed from 1861, under Victor Emmanuel II of Sardinia, until the referendum that created the Italian Republic in 1946, when the monarchy was abolished. And here's an interesting fact: because of the obvious tensions this created with the Vatican, all the roads were laid out so you couldn't see St Peter's Basilica from any of them.

Prati is really worth a visit and is a great place to stay. Quiet, but close to everything.

There's also the Church of the Sacro Cuoro dei Suffragio (the Sacred Heart of the Suffrage), which contains the Museum of the Souls of Purgatory. Here you will find exhibits such as fingerprints on a bible said to be signs of spirits in the netherworld trying to contact the living, though they could just as easily be signs of someone having eaten some chips and not wiped their hands.

The district boasts lots of charming small trattorias and osterias set into small archways and niches on the side streets. These are refreshingly 'un-touristy' and reassuringly full of locals. We did attempt to eat in one such establishment, which had about twenty covers and was run by an aged husband and wife who clearly found the whole thing unbearably stressful. The proprietor was nothing if not welcoming but told us to stand close to an elderly Italian gentleman who was contentedly dining alone. We were informed that he would be finishing soon and then we could be seated. We asked why we couldn't just take the empty spot on the other side of the room but were told that wasn't possible as it was a table for four. Which it wasn't. It was two tables for two pushed together, and therefore easily separated.

Arlo was being kept on a tight leash throughout these discussions and I could tell he was getting restive. He takes his time deciding whether to sit or lie down, as he wants to make sure it's somewhere we're going to be hanging around for a while. Otherwise, it's not worth the effort of furling and unfurling those eight-inch legs. He was perusing the premises and thinking that any of the available tables would be acceptable to crouch under and affix his nonpareil cute-face to ensure maximum morsels. I was thinking pretty much the same thing and gestured to our charming yet exasperated host to indicate this. To no avail. He remained insistent that the occupier of the table he'd earmarked for us was just finishing up. We pointed out that this stoically unruffled roué had about three-quarters of a bottle of wine left and had just taken delivery of his pudding

With growing frustration and visible high blood pressure, the Basil Fawlty of the Roman restaurant scene then approached said diner and barked: 'Vai via!' which translates as: 'Go away!'

Looking up from his tiramisu, the carefree cove calmly replied: 'No!'

Remarkable.

Glancing at my wristwatch as if remembering some urgent appointment, we made our feeble excuses and left.

A few hundred feet down the block we came across a similarly quaint noshery where the patron had introduced a revolutionary scheme whereby newcomers were shown to seats that weren't already occupied.

It was a system that seemed to be working well.

The house Arlo mentioned was the Villa Farnesina, which is famous for boasting ceiling frescoes of Cupid and Psyche by Raphael no less. (Don't forget to look up, Fiona.)

He did have to be carried, or, to use the rather lovely Italian phrase for 'in arms', *in bracchia*, which when said properly sounds very like you're being encouraged to embrace your dog. Sweet.

Arlo seemed delighted not to have to walk for a while and indeed received a good deal of cooing attention from other visitors, some of whom may later have reflected that they had paid rather too much attention to a lethargic cavapoo than some of the finest handiwork of a master of High Renaissance art.

It did take a bewilderingly long time to get in, though – he's right. There was just one ticket window with a single unsmiling bloke issuing entrance vouchers from Rome's slowest computer. Each transaction involved him looking confusedly at the screen for several minutes before printing off the passes with a sense of relief. I could understand this if he was booking complex and varied travel documents but everyone going into the Villa Farnesina just wanted the same thing. A ticket for the villa. I mean, how hard can that be to organise?

The villa was built between 1506 and 1510 for Agostino Chigi, who was the Pope's banker. Well, I'm sure that was a lucrative gig and probably involved a stupidly big bonus, like all financial people seem to think they deserve for doing the job they're already lavishly paid to do. So, as you can imagine, it's quite an impressive gaff. I was particularly taken with the artistic skill and vision of an artwork depicting some ancient blade-sharpening men-at-work, while also being relieved that I hadn't had a job as a knife-grinder in a time before they invented trousers.

Funnily enough, the wanton display of male genitalia is something that has been controversial in the Roman art world. A bloke called Daniele da Volterra is also known as *Il Braghettone* or 'the breeches-maker' as he was hired to paint pantaloons on to several figures in *The Last Judgement* at the Sistine Chapel during the Counter-Reformation.

Oddly, the dogs of Trastevere do seem to be a bit tetchy. Perhaps it's because they're hot and having to negotiate crowds but it also can't help that there is broken glass everywhere. Arlo is right to point this out.

They love a broken bottle here. It is a bit of a mystery. Where does it all come from? It's as if after drinking a beer, every single person cheerfully smashes the bottle on the street. They don't, from what I can see, but somehow they manage to get shards all over the place. Perhaps if I go back to oversee the opening of an outlet for my world-famous DogClogs™ the protection for paws will result in moderation in the mentality of the municipal mutts. In the meantime, perhaps a couple of bottle banks?

The Mouth of Truth
and Meat Products

Today we embarked on the biggest waste of time since we got here. We stood in a line for about four or five hours to see a grid. I know, right? And then They stuck my paw in it and took a photo. Of me and a stupid drain!

Humans! What are they like?

Fortunately things got a lot better after that but then how could they not?

We went to the Campo de Fury where they have a great market that sells loads of lovely meat products such as mortadella, prosciutto, speck, coppa and guanciale.

Well, I say it got better, but not until after I'd been set upon by a well-snappy mongrel. I mean, I know wolves played a part in the foundation of Rome but this was getting ridiculous.

I guess that's why that square is called what it's called as that snarling cur was well furious about something.

Thankfully, after I yelped in shock and indignation, I did get some decent meaty mouthfuls by way of compensation because everyone felt sorry for me.

It was hard to say exactly what it was but if I had to guess I would say bresaola maybe.

It was tasty but I would have enjoyed it more if that bloke hadn't been screaming in pain throughout the whole meal. I know I squealed when that mangy mutt attacked me but I calmed down when I'd been fed.

Why didn't someone give some grub to that chap to shut him up?

Why indeed? The fellow in question wasn't actually in pain. He was a busker singing Nirvana's 'Smells Like Teen Spirit'. To be fair, he was making a fairly decent fist of it and was at least backing himself on guitar. Quite a few street 'performers' in Rome are just singing to a backing track. That's not busking, it's karaoke, and no one should expect to be paid for that.

So our grunge minstrel was playing by the rules and his voice was suitably raucous and would have sounded terrific if backed by a full band in a sweaty club. But it's not really what you want to hear in a lantern-lit piazza while you pick at what Arlo correctly identified as bresaola and sip your Prosecco, and even Kurt Cobain would concede that. I really like to think that if he and Courtney had been holding hands at a small table-for-two with a red and white chequered tablecloth they'd have paid the lad a few euros to go away and hoped, like the rest of us, for a little gentle accordion music. As I say, this guy put his all into it as if he really was suffering for his art, even if he wasn't suffering quite as much as the rest of us. However, to keep things in perspective when it comes to suffering, there is a statue in the middle of the square of the philosopher and poet Giordano Bruno who was burned at the stake there on 17 February 1600 for, among other things, his pantheistic views. He maintained that reality, nature and the universe are at least as important as any supreme entity. And that sealed his fate. Ironically, ten minutes' walk away is the Pantheon, which was built as a temple to multiple gods, thereby celebrating pantheism in the most ostentatious way possible. Funny old world, isn't it?

This effigy is sited in what is indeed pronounced as the 'campo de fury', although the correct spelling is Campo de' Fiori, the 'field of the flowers', as it was a meadow in the Middle Ages.

Arlo is spot on about the quality of produce on offer in the market there. They flog good, fresh produce right in the heart of the city at really reasonable prices. Of course, it's not without the smattering of tat that's freely available in all mercantile zones and in the myriad circular kiosks and tabac stalls you find on every other street corner.

Here you can avail yourself of fridge magnets, coasters, bobble-heads (I know, I know), Roma baseball caps, the same paintings of the Colosseum as the street 'artists' but at least they're not pretending to have created them, Sistine Chapel ceiling mugs (we bought two) and papal calendars. Sometimes not even of the current pontiff. Interesting. Who's in the market for a Pope almanac but with a previous Holy Father centre stage? Pope John Paul II, you know, the Polish one, still seems very much in demand. Pope Benedict XVI, you know, the German one, not so much. Personally I was after one dedicated to Pope Innocent X but they didn't go back to the 1640s apparently. *Why him?* I hear you ask. Well, not only was he immortalised by Diego Velázquez in 1650, but he was also the inspiration for the 'Screaming Pope' pictures of Francis Bacon. He did about fifty of them. And still had time to paint his own hair with shoe polish. That made for quite a strong look.

The other calendars that are notable in their ubiquity are ones of, for want of a better expression, fit priests. That's odd, don't you think? Marketing as sex symbols guys who've sworn themselves to a life of celibacy.

Arlo was, as usual, wrong about the time we spent in a queue. We were there about twenty minutes. He's kind of right when he said we stood in line to see a grid, though.

The Mouth of Truth (*Bocca della Verità*) is a familiar tourist

stop and photo opportunity. It's a large marble mask dating from
the first century AD and probably was once used as a drain cover.
Some say it's on the site of a former meat market and was used to
direct the flow of blood after animal slaughter, while others claim
it's a humble sewer lid. This seems the most likely as it dates from
the reign of the seventh and last of the ancient kings of Rome,
Tarquin the Superb. And how marvellous to be remembered as
that, eh? So what was it that made him so celebrated for all eter-
nity? Well, he was certainly very big on drainage. Rather like the
Joseph Bazalgette of antiquity, he instigated works that cleaned
up the streets of the Eternal City no end in the sixth century BC.
And you can see how important this might have been. All very
well conquering and fighting and doing heroic stuff to build up
the empire but you don't want to come back and be ankle-deep
in excrement while going about your business. Especially in open-
toed sandals. Superb? You bet. Counter to that is the legend that
so unpopular was Tarquin that when he died they chucked his
body into the Tiber and the gradual build-up of silt over him led
to the creation of Tiber Island. So maybe not so Superb after all.

The mask itself is thought to be the Titan god Oceanus and you
traditionally stick your hand, or arm, in its mouth. Legend has it
that if you are a liar it will bite down and sever a limb, or at least
a finger or two.

It notably features in a scene with Audrey Hepburn and
Gregory Peck in the classic 1953 film *Roman Holiday*, and though
Arlo had no way of knowing this, being more of a *La Dolce Vita*
aficionado, it was good to see him enjoying his own re-creation
of that. He did give me one of those slightly disdainful looks that
made me question what I was doing when I placed his paw in the
jaw but it seemed important at the time.

Interestingly, this famed gob was said to have been used to

check on the faithfulness of wives. Not husbands, just wives. That gives you some indication of where the battle of the sexes was at in those days.

Bella put her arm in and pulled the requisite grimace for the camera and came out fully intact.

Euphorically un-cuckolded, I was able to carry on the rest of the day with a certain lightness of step.

A Buggy Ride to Meet Moses

I suppose when you stay somewhere for a long time some days are going to be rubbish, and this was one of them. It started off with a walk, which was okay, but then glancing through a big gate thing I could see some really lovely gardens that went on for miles. Great, I thought. Off-the-lead time. No such luck. We just kept on walking down some boring streets, which made no sense to me. Why plod along pavements when you can run on grass?

Anyway, if that was all a bit dull, things were about to get a good deal worse. We then sat on two plastic chairs on wheels. It was like a car but one that had quite a lot of bits missing. Like doors, for a start.

As if that wasn't bad enough, there was no seat for me so I just had to sit on Her lap. It was pretty uncomfortable and when we got on the road it was just shaky and totally rubbish. Also it was dead, dead windy.

Now, I know there are some showy-off dogs who like to ride along with their heads out of the window but I'm not one of them. I like everything closed and the heater on and a comfy seat and perhaps a couple of rugs or blankets, thanks very much. This was just torture and when we went through a tunnel and everything got dark and really, really loud, I had absolutely had enough.

Eventually we got to a boring square where there was nothing to see and nothing happened and it was really hot.

Then we had another bone-shaking trip in this contraption before I got home for some salmon and a lovely long kip on the sofa with some rugs and blankets, thanks very much.

As I said – a rubbish day.

Well, not for us, but I could see why it might have seemed like it to him.

I was only too well aware of his tugging towards the extensive gardens. At first, he tried to pull in that direction without making eye contact. Such was his determination. However, once that tactic failed he looked up at me with the face he uses to induce me to feed him more of my dinner than is strictly sensible. I'm usually powerless to resist this expression of longing but there was a good reason for not giving in to him on this occasion.

These were the gardens of the Vatican, which run to 57 acres. You might think this sounds pretty big and you'd be right. It's the biggest garden in the world as a percentage of the nation it's located in as Vatican City is an independent state of just 120 acres. It's the smallest country on earth and is about one fifth the size of Central Park in New York. So it is a garden covering more or less half of the country. However, Arlo's dream of capering around the pontiff's magnolias would never be realised as dogs are not allowed in there. I felt for him and wanted to explore myself. I was particularly intrigued by the mysterious buildings tantalisingly glimpsed through the gates. One was a big shed. I imagine that's where His Holiness keeps his patio furniture in winter.

We hired a small electric buggy for the day from a nice chap called Peter in a part of town next to the Vatican called Borgo. It had a top speed of 25 km/h and that feels quite nippy given that the average speed of Rome traffic is 20 km/h. The first thing Peter said to me before I drove away was: 'Forget your polite Anglo-Saxon driving etiquette. Go where you want, when you want. Everyone else does.'

If this sounds vaguely terrifying it quickly became totally liberating. If you saw a space on the road you just nipped into it. And nobody gave you grief for it as it was exactly the way they expected you to drive. An angry bus driver did more or less buffet me out of the way as I was blocking access to his stop, which was fair enough. An irate white van man came up close behind me and leaned on his horn, but I took this as a sign of general irritation and impatience with the congestion rather than a personal message to me. I could have been wrong but what did I care? As soon as a gap the size of a wheely bin opened up I was through it and off.

There are so many varieties of tiny city vehicles in Rome that you really don't see at home. The Yoyo cars are really cute but I was particularly drawn to the Renault Twizy. This is a sort of car/motor scooter hybrid. There are two seats but one behind the other. You can purchase them in the UK and I am sorely tempted to get one for me and Arlo to buzz around Knutsford. Bella thinks it's a ridiculous idea. I daresay she's right but that doesn't mean I've absolutely ruled it out. What's more likely to persuade me out of it is that Arlo might hate it as much as he did the rented go-kart. He really is a cosseted townie who is quite happy to experience the great outdoors but likes the journey there and back to be comfortable. Cushions, blankets and heaters are the least he expects.

The 'boring square' Arlo was so unimpressed by was indeed a bit dull at first glance. It was clogged up with cars and unforgiving in the midday sun. It did boast yet another spectacular fountain but it was on a high pedestal and, other than providing a bit of shady respite beneath its sculpted bowl, wasn't of massive interest to me let alone him.

However, the piazza is also home to the Basilica of San Pietro in Vincoli. Translated from the Latin, this literally means St Peter in Chains, which he was. Twice, in fact, if you go along with this stuff. He was thrown in the clink in Jerusalem by Herod for preaching about Jesus. That got him manacled but, being well connected with the big fellow upstairs, an angel came and freed him the night before his trial. Phew! It's not what you know but who you know.

He was also incarcerated in the Mamertine Prison in the Forum by Nero, who, like Herod, wasn't renowned for his tolerance and forgiving nature. He was shackled there too. If you're a believer and were wondering about the whereabouts of these two sets of chains and hoping against hope they weren't melted down for scrap, then you're in luck. Because they're here. In a gilded glass box in the central nave just before you get to the altar. And because it's both fetters, they qualify as a 'double relic'. How about that? Rather like the amps in *This is Spinal Tap* going up to eleven, this relic goes up to two. That's one louder than a regular relic. Having seen the imprint of his knees, these felt like the icing on the canonical cake.

But as if that wasn't enough, this basilica, though rather un-prepossessing from the outside by Roman standards, is home to another wonder. I suppose the effect looking at St Peter's chains has on you depends on the depth of your faith. That's not really a consideration when you move to the far right of the church to stand in front of Michelangelo's tomb of Pope Julius II. Yes, it is full of religious figures and symbolism but as an exercise in artistic creation it is unfathomable. Like the Caravaggios, and again entry here is free, you can't help thinking about divine intervention.

Firstly, it is huge. It is a floor-to-ceiling piece, and in churches ceilings tend to be pretty high. Centre stage is the colossal figure of Moses with the late pontiff reclining in a rather louche posture above him. There are seven full-size statues in the work plus an infant and four busts of bearded figures acting as caryatids holding up the top deck. The level of detail is just beyond comprehension. How is it possible for anyone to have got a block of stone, a hammer, chisel and some stepladders and ended up with this? Mind you, it took him a while. Forty years in fact, from 1505 to 1545. How Julius felt about it is uncertain as he died in 1513.

Forty years though! Does anyone work on anything for forty years any more, except for the Sagrada Família in Barcelona? But when you think about it, it's the blink of an eye. People have been standing in front of the tomb in wonder for nearly five hundred years and will do so for evermore. And you don't even have to wait for the light to come on.

Overwhelming though it is, it's also worth noting that what we see is only a fraction of the original plan, which was for it to be installed in St Peter's and include forty-seven statues. So this monolithic masterpiece is actually very much the scaled-down version.

It being a place of worship, Arlo had to hang around on the boring square while we took turns to go inside. When I sat on the steps with him, he kept looking up at me with his head slightly tilted and a quizzical look in his eye.

'I know,' I said. 'You're still thinking about the gardens, aren't you?'

Knowing him as I do, though, I can't imagine he would have wanted me to miss seeing Moses and his mates. He also had to wait outside St Peter's so we could stand in awe in front of another of Michelangelo's triumphs, but at least that time he got compensated with salami from a panino, from which he had all the filling. I was planning to share it with him but once he'd had all the meat I was less tempted by the limp baguette impregnated with grease so chucked it in the bin. Even so, I felt it was fair enough because he never got to see *La Pietà*.

The *Pietà* is in the first chapel on the right as you go in and is the sculpture of the Virgin Mary cradling an adult Christ after he has been taken down from the cross. What you're actually seeing is a partial resurrection itself. It's behind a screen now as, in 1972, Laszlo Toth attacked and damaged it with a geologist's hammer while claiming to be the reincarnation of Jesus. He removed most of an arm and the nose before being wrestled to the ground. It's been restored, of course, but it remains a deeply disturbing incident. Just imagine that Jesus returns after two millennia and the first thing on his 'to-do' list is to vandalise a statue of his mum. You'd have to call that a disappointment, wouldn't you? Rather as if he'd turned up heavily tattooed, wearing a baseball cap backwards and munching a cheeseburger.

But *La Pietà* is one of the wonders of the world. Look closely at the folds on Mary's veil and gown. How is it possible for anyone to have created those effects using a simple tool on stone? Not only that, Michelangelo was in his early twenties when he did it. Then again, age doesn't really matter. No one else, except Bernini perhaps, could get anywhere near it if they lived to be a thousand. So how are we to explain it? Ultimately there are only three possible answers. The first is magic, so we can discount that. The second is that we are encountering the hand of the greatest artistic genius ever to have lived. Well, quite possibly. The third is that he was guided directly by God. It's the closest thing there is to physical proof of a higher power that I know of.

Incidentally, you can also visit Michelangelo's house up the hill on Janiculum Walk. Well, kind of. What you actually see is the facade of his former residence, which is pretty much uncelebrated and often obscured by four or five guaranteed-MOT-failure vehicles with very limited scrap value parked on the forecourt. Arlo had a sniff around the bald tyres, no doubt dreading that he was going to be hanging around for a while as we took turns wandering around in there. He needn't have worried. You can't get inside. Michelangelo used to live near the Capitoline Hill but when demolition works took place in 1872 the front of the residence was saved and recycled only for the replacement building to be knocked down in the thirties. Once again, the frontage was saved and in 1941 was moved to its present location, where it apparently conceals a large water tank. It seems a bit sad somehow but then setting up some kind of museum there is a very tall order. There are only eighteen fully attributed Michelangelo statues in existence so getting one of those is going to be tricky.

There are a few more of his paintings knocking about but most of those are firmly in situ in the Sistine Chapel. Oddly, Michelangelo didn't really think of himself as a painter and counted not only sculpture but also architecture, poetry and madrigal composition as higher on his prodigious list of talents. That must have led to an interesting conversation when the Vatican centrepiece was under discussion:

'Could you rattle off some paintings for the ceiling here, Mike?'

'Well, it's not really what I do but I'll have a go. You can always paint it out if you don't like it.'

They didn't, Fiona.

Two Haircuts

'Me and Him up a thousand steps on the balcony of our little house.'

I went for a stylish Italian haircut today. I hate having my hair cut.

The lady doing it was very nice and had a big smile and lots of curly hair so that put my mind at ease a bit.

She had a certificate on the wall as well to show she was a properly qualified stylist. And a picture of a little dog under a hairdryer.

Nevertheless I don't like being left somewhere with someone I don't know because I'm wondering when someone will come back to collect me.

Anyway, it turned out all right.

I had a horrid shampoo with horrid water and then a blow dry. It looked great.

Everybody said I looked really young and cute.

And d'you know what? It's been really hot here and so it felt great to have all that fur off and to be able to run about in the Villa Sciarra without panting so much.

My haircut cost about €45, which I think is about the same as at home.

His cost €10, which seems like quite a big price difference but then I've got a lot more hair than Him.

Fair point.

Obviously my haircut was also Italian, though I don't think anyone would have called it stylish.

In contrast to the dog groomer, my guy seemed initially quite surly and had an elaborate white mullet-ish coiffure. Old school.

He had a certificate hanging up, too. And a calendar on which a dark-haired woman was easing herself out of some bikini bottoms. Again, of the old school.

Unlike Arlo, I was out of there in about ten minutes but I too had a blow dry, for the first time in about thirty years. It looked like a combover.

Perhaps unsurprisingly, no one said I looked really young. Or indeed cute, though clearly it would take a lot more than a Roman scalping to achieve that.

I guess being shorn must feel terrific for a dog though, right? They must be so relieved not to be overheating any more.

In Knutsford I quite often see people in those really expensive pure-down puffer coats that cost upwards of a grand. They must be boiling. If you're crossing the Arctic Circle one of those jackets would be ideal. For having a latte in Cheshire, not so much. They're the oversized-4×4-offroad-SUV-on-narrow-urban-street of outerwear. But you've spent many hundreds of pounds on the heavily insulated anorak thing and so you have to wear it. Imagine the relief, though, when you can take it off. You can also achieve this effect by not putting it on. Or indeed wasting your money on it.

Of course, what to wear isn't a problem for dogs. I do envy them that, especially when it comes to packing. I'm one for making lists before I go away so I don't forget stuff.

Arlo can't do that but then it doesn't matter if he forgets things as there's nothing he needs to remember.

In many ways this proves that dogs are much better suited to life on earth than we are. They can go anywhere without needing anything no matter for how long or how far away.

'What's that you say? We're going to the pub for an hour? Yep, I'm ready.'

Alternatively: 'What's that you say? We're going to Rome for a few months? Yep, I'm ready.'

Having said that, they can't drive so let's call it a draw.

The Dying City and
the Sacred Wood

Aren't cars brilliant?

We went in ours for quite a long time today, and here's one of the many things that confuses me about humans. They drive through lots of lovely countryside with trees and hills and fields that look great for walks before finishing up in a stupidly busy place with loads of buildings. Not only that, but when we do finally get out for a stroll in the stupidly busy areas we sometimes hang about by a wall for no reason at all. I've no choice but to wait patiently hoping that something might happen, but why keep stopping at places where there's nothing to sniff, chase or look at?

Eventually we walked to the town square where there was the possibility of some action at last. Cats. Lots of them. I like to think of myself as really mellow but I absolutely hate cats. I know some dogs live with cats and they learn to get on fine. I don't live in a house like that and so I haven't moved beyond detesting all felines on sight. I'm not proud of it. For one thing, seeing one and then straining at the leash, whimpering and barking isn't very dignified, is it? How can I stop it though? Is canine counselling for anger management issues an option?

It's weird. I may not like squirrels or swans either, but most animals I'm fine with. In that stupidly busy place they sometimes had donkey rides and I'd have been fine with that.

Anyway, we then went to a nice-looking forest but, get this, dogs weren't allowed in! I mean, seriously? It's a forest. That is insane.

On the other hand, I wasn't all that bothered because it was raining and They were also talking about some funny stones in the woods but, really, how funny can stones be?

We finished off going to another stupidly busy place full of buildings and stared at another wall for a bit. Give me strength. Thank goodness there were more stupid cats to threaten or I'd have been bored out of my mind.

This second 'stupidly busy place' was the resplendently preserved city of Orvieto.

And the wall incurring Arlo's disinterest?

The facade of Orvieto Cathedral. Gaze on it in wonder. It is one of the towering artistic achievements of the late Middle Ages. It features carvings, statues, bronze doors, an intricate rose window and breathtaking golden mosaics. The original ones were created between 1350 and 1390, but most of the ones we see today were created in the sixteenth century by the local artist Cesare Nebbia, who also has some paintings in the Gallery of Maps at the Vatican.

The first 'stupidly busy place' was one of the most spectacular hilltop villages you will ever see.

It is called Civita di Bagnoregio and was cut off from the rest of the town of Bagnoregio by an earthquake in 1695. It's an amazing place to visit, though our day didn't get off to the most promising of starts. The ticket machine at the car park didn't work. I asked in the visitor centre if I could pay there but the frosty woman behind the counter gave me a blunt 'NO' without glancing up from her computer screen. You do wonder why people who clearly hate people take jobs dealing with people, don't you?

The waitress serving coffee in the small café next door was perfectly efficient but averse to smiling.

We then had to wait for a shuttle bus to take us to the marooned village and thought we'd use the facilities. This cost €1, but having put the money in the slot, the barrier failed to open. We tried again with the same result. Summoning up my meagre reserves of pluck, I returned to the tourist office to explain our predicament and I'm glad I did because otherwise I would have had to manage without a shrug of total indifference. In desperation, I clambered over the turnstile to see what kind of toilet a euro gets you in those parts. No seat or paper, as we'd come to expect. Here, though, there was the added bonus of there being no obvious way of flushing either. Great. Money well spent. I did consider reporting the conditions back to the information point but thought I might come out with a bloodied nose.

Arlo casually and copiously relieved himself on an evidently aromatic corner of the tourist office. I took some solace from that.

Bladders duly emptied, we boarded the shuttle and within ten minutes caught our first sighting of the Civita.

It is a cluster of ancient buildings hugging each other on a precipitous mound with a church tower rising from its midst. You reach the Civita via a steep footbridge rising up as if approaching the ramparts of a medieval castle before entering a pleasing town square of rough-hewn walls, wisteria, shutters, castellations, cats and a smattering of visitors enjoying an al fresco lunch. It is said the village only has sixteen full-time residents. If this is so, then it seemed like every one of them had opened a bar or café. And why not? What other options could possibly be available to you there to make a living?

It's also unclear how long any of it will continue to be possible.

It is called 'the dying city' as its unstable footings, constantly subjected to erosion, make its future uncertain.

Having said all that, its future has been uncertain since 1695 so if it is dying, it's taking quite a long time to die completely.

The views from there are spectacular but Arlo wouldn't know this. We were on one of the many vertigo-inducing terraces at the edge of the town affording a panorama over the undulating hills, steep cliffs, vine and olive groves, and cypress and umbrella pine trees of the Lazio countryside. It was stunning. For us. Arlo was at ground level, looking at a wall. I did keep leaning down and patting him on the head to try and indicate that we would be on our way soon. I even picked him up so he could gaze into the middle distance but he really didn't seem bothered. Dogs don't do 'views', do they? And I guess a collection of tightly grouped historical architectural gems is much the same as a new-build estate if all you're really interested in is chasing cats.

And the donkeys? Every June in the 'dying city' they re-create Siena's celebrated Palio in the minuscule main piazza with donkeys. Who doesn't love a donkey? In fact, in Orvieto there's a gallery exclusively selling the works of the fantasy artist Umberto Verdirosi. Apparently he has also been an actor, poet, sculptor and philosopher, and donkeys often appear in his paintings. He is very keen to explain his work and one line I picked out of his musings was: 'Only by being a donkey have I attained wisdom.'

Having found that pretty profound I delved further into his 'mission statement'. This didn't involve all that much research because it is posted at length outside his shop. Consider this: 'It is not me who wrote my fairy tale ... it was life. Be aware that you are the actors, all I did was painting you.'

Well, quite. I took a lot from that and it made me realise that in this fairy tale you should be aware that Arlo is the author and all I did was writing it.

Should you want to gain a deeper understanding of the

thoughts of Verdirosi you'll be pleased to know he's written ten books to explain his innermost thinking and theories. Thank goodness for that, eh?

The forest in question was the sacred wood – Sacro Bosco – in the shadow of another hilltop settlement, the village of Bomarzo. And the funny stones did turn out to be quite funny.

The noble Orsini family have a palace up there and in the sixteenth century Prince Vicino Orsini decided to build a park of follies on the estate. Accordingly you will find a lush wooded glade of babbling streams and gentle hillocks populated by a series of deeply odd and surprising statues. In truth, they are kind of rudimentary if you're comparing them to Bernini's handiwork, but that only adds to their unsettling presence somehow. They're generally about twenty to thirty feet high and there are about forty of them. They give you a little checklist so you can make sure you've seen the elephant with a castle on its back, the tortoise with an obelisk on its shell, various oversized nymphs, a dragon devouring a dog, a fountain with Pegasus on the top, a crooked house, assorted muses and a couple of burly chaps turning each other upside down in what I very much hoped was a violent rather than passionate embrace. There are also a couple of grottos with entrances made to resemble large ghoulish faces. You can go inside one of them, rather like that bloke living inside Diego Maradona's head in Naples.

It's an endearingly strange place but Arlo wasn't allowed in. To be honest, if he had been admitted I don't think he would have been impressed. It's possible he could have been traumatised by happening across the spectacle of one of his forebears being scoffed by a fire-breathing beast of myth. I did offer him a constitutional around the rain-lashed car park but he preferred to look at me grumpily with downturned mouth from the comfort of his back-seat velveteen crib, making it clear that he was going nowhere.

Why they don't let dogs in is a mystery. What possible damage could they do to a forest path littered with sculptural peculiarities that have been standing there for several hundred years?

It's hardly the Sistine Chapel.

Port of Rome, Belly of Rome

We went to an odd spot today where people were selling things under a big glass roof. There were lots of little shops and I quite liked that because some would be selling boring stuff like hats and scarves and gloves for feet and stuff but round every corner there would be a good meaty place where the smells were brilliant. It was flipping hot though. I was quite glad to lie down and have a drink but as I was starting to chill out this crowd of people started wailing at the tops of their voices. People are a bit shouty here, and wave their hands about a lot. The dogs are barky too, so it can be quite noisy generally, but this was ridiculous. What a racket. I'd have put my fingers in my ears if I'd had any. Fingers that is. I do have ears.

After that we went on a bit of a walk and guess what? We looked at another pile of stones! You'd have thought we'd have seen enough of those by now, wouldn't you? You've seen one pile of stones, you've seen them all.

It might have been my imagination but I thought I could smell the sea even though I couldn't see it.

It might also have been my imagination to imagine that I have the capacity for imagination.

We then went to a really weird place that I got a funny feeling about. I couldn't put my finger on why. Not least because, as I've said, I don't have any fingers. Pay attention.

They took turns going into a big shed but I wasn't allowed in.

Not even *in bracchia*. This seemed a bit stupid because it was a blooming shed. It's not like it had nice carpets or posh floors with pictures or anything.

So I was quite pleased to get away from there and set off home.

On our way back a man with a brush smiled and stroked me, which was sweet, and quite unusual here, but then he asked us for some money. That was a bit bonkers. I would have thought that he should pay us if anything because he could feel how soft I was and we didn't get anything from him for what we paid him. I'll never understand humans if I live to be a hundred. Which is about a thousand in human years, I think.

Way off. It's about fifteen.

This street interaction is something that happens quite a lot here. An unemployed person will temporarily take over a stretch of pavement and sweep and clean it in return for a donation. Presumably they are targeting local residents who might well appreciate not having to be careful to avoid broken glass and canine deposits. I think it's a good idea. How much more likely would you be to drop a coin in the hat of someone doing something useful rather than just lounging about? I'm in no way making light of the people who are forced to live on the streets but I do applaud these guys for trying to make small improvements to the urban scene. It's a sort of self-generated community service.

The 'odd spot' was the Mercato di Testaccio and is well worth a visit. It is an authentic local market full of delicious fresh produce, tasty street food, cheap stylish clothing and various nick-nacks and *objets d'art*. Some tat as well. Bobbleheads are in evidence.

Being a bustling marketplace under a glass roof it was pretty high on the decibel level but this was increased tenfold in a marvellous and unexpected way. The 'racket' Arlo refers to was actually an extraordinarily precise and powerful performance of the 'Dies irae' from Mozart's *Requiem* by a first-rate choir. It wasn't a concert as such but part of a public protest against the privatisation of the Post Office. Guys, come on. You have nothing to fear. Nothing stays the same forever. Our Post Office was reorganised yonks ago and it's worked like a dream. Some of the executives who ran ours have left their jobs now so we can send them over if you like.

As for the stones, well I know what he means. From ground level they must all look pretty much the same, and if you were a teenager on holiday with your parents being dragged round these places ad nauseam then you would be thinking along the same lines, and also planning to be really sulky to get your own back while counting down the months until you could get served in bars.

It's also possible that with his advanced sense of smell Arlo could detect a distant whiff of brine despite us being landlocked because this 'pile of stones' was in fact part of the harbour of the original Port of Rome.

Nearby is another Roman hill, called Monte Testaccio. This one was formed not by natural phenomena but by the build-up of olive oil jars that were shipped down the river and discarded after use. They were very much the free plastic bags of their day. There are thought to be about six million of them under there, dating back maybe as far as the first century BC.

From there we strolled on to a complex of part-renovated pavilions called Mattatoio. I'm not surprised that Arlo felt uneasy. Animals haven't enjoyed going there much over the years.

The site is now home to art galleries and installation spaces

along with a drama academy and music school. But its history is
pretty grisly. Dubbed 'the belly of Rome', it was opened in 1890
as the largest slaughterhouse in Europe and remained operational
until 1975. It is huge and consists of rows of long, straight, low-
level industrial barns surrounded by the rusting remains of a
pulley system on overhead tracks designed to transport carcasses.

What it must have been like to work there is scarcely imaginable. In fact, though, jobs there were highly valued and often
passed down through family generations. And the perks, though
malodorous, were not to be sniffed at. Thanks to a system called
'*quinto quarto*', employees were given free access to the unwanted
offal and offcuts. This meant they could go home with a sizeable
'lucky bag' of intestines, brains and nerves. Yum. Though Arlo
would have happily tucked in, I daresay. Pampered he may be, but
he's still a dog and so has some disgusting inbred tendencies. A
roll in some fox poo and a *quinto quarto* platter he would consider
a grand day out.

This will be an amazing space and it is great to see it being
repurposed but, right now, it has an unsettling atmosphere.
Poppies grow in the pens where once animals nearing their demise
were held and the deep, rumbling sub-bass emanating from the location of a large-scale video exhibit made you feel you were on the
set of a film you would never really want to see. To make it even
more macabre there is a museum of pathological anatomy there,
where you can see over two thousand exhibits from surgeries and
autopsies including 'nine hundred malformed hearts'.

Or, as the original workforce called it, lunch.

Given that many hundreds of thousands of animals had been
herded through there over the years it did seem a bit odd that, like
the 'sacred wood', dogs weren't allowed in.

Disgruntled though Arlo clearly was, I did leave him with Bella while I went to view an exhibition called *Urlo – Vibrazioni Urbane* by the Roman artist Andrea Sampaolo.

It consisted of large colourful abstract canvases and small gangs of similarly vivid humanoid figures labelled 'hominids'. I found it powerful and affecting even though I was struggling to see the connection it had to Rome's 'dialectic between light and dark'.

I read with interest that: 'Urlo breaks the order, invades the social space and brings it to a process of change. It is a political dimension far broader than ideology. A deep political essence that calls into question the original human nature.'

I've gone over this several times and am still no closer to extracting a meaning from it, but that didn't stop me getting a lot from the show.

I was just sorry that Arlo and Urlo didn't have their own dialectic.

EUR (pronounced ay-oor)

Today started off quite well. We waited down our street in front of that house with lots of tables in it that always smells great.

After about an hour, during which lots of passing people kept waving at us, a friendly man came and let us get in his car, and we set off for a place I soon decided I had no real interest in visiting. For a start, there wasn't much grass there. It goes without saying that there were lots of stones but at least someone had made an effort to stack them into proper towers instead of just leaving them lying around in messy piles. There were a lot of big concrete boxes with windows in them too and it was dead, dead hot, so not much fun at all. She hadn't come with us and I think She'd made a good decision.

Some of the buildings had lots of people outside who looked really serious and busy with their jobs of smoking. They were really good at it. I imagine they'd been doing it for years and had learned how to puff really, really hard. Good on them for putting in a shift. I hate slackers, don't you?

Some other buildings seemed empty but humans must have been there recently to make sure there was plenty of smashed glass to avoid.

Anyway, then we went to get on a tram that went into a tunnel but nearly got on the wrong one and had to come out again and cross the road to the other side. And that was when we nearly got run into by a bin on wheels.

You know me and Him are great together when it's just the two of us but I sometimes feel a bit safer if She's there too.

I don't think She would have got so close to that stupid bin-car thing.

Well, harsh but not totally beyond the realms of plausibility.

We did take the Metro but, initially, and somewhat inevitably, going in the wrong direction. So we did have to return to street level and cross a busy dual carriageway. This did indeed result in a near-miss with a Fiat Panda. I know what he means by 'a bin on wheels'. I can only imagine that the Fiat design team were called into the boardroom in Turin sometime in the late seventies and given the following brief:

'Guys, we want you to come up with a car that most closely resembles a skip.'

They really pulled that one off and no mistake.

The day had begun with a cab ride. We were picked up from a small bistro called L'Osteria della Trippa. You can probably hazard a guess at what that means. It's basically boasting that their house speciality is stomach lining. As discussed, tripe seems irrationally popular here and even among people who don't work at abattoirs. It's on every menu and was ordered at a nice eatery called Zi Umberto in the heart of Trastevere by a pal of mine who'd dropped by for a couple of days. The waiters there are nothing if not sharp and witty, and our server expressed surprise at the dish ordered.

'A friend of mine told me that when in Rome you should try the tripe,' said the nervous diner.

The riposte came without missing a beat: 'Are you sure he's your friend?'

We all tried some. The verdict? Let's just say that Arlo did quite well that night. He actually got into a slight tizzy under the table as morsels were coming at him from four different directions and he didn't know which way to turn next. The fact that he'd been dismissive of rubbery food earlier in his stay seemed to have slipped his mind as he gratefully gobbled most of an adult portion of intestine à la Roma.

Our taxi actually came in under four minutes and our destination was EUR. Oh, and the locals weren't waving at us. They were definitely waving but people here do that all the time. Usually when they are on their hands-free smartphones. Interestingly, although, as I've pointed out, Romans seem to eschew this technology when driving, they heartily embrace it while on foot. Go figure that!

EUR stands for Esposizione Universale Roma, and was the proposed site of the 1942 World's Fair, which Mussolini was very much looking forward to hosting as a major propaganda exercise before the Second World War got in the way. It is about half an hour's ride outside the city walls and is like nowhere else in the environs of Rome. Its principal buildings are huge statements of totalitarian neoclassicism. The intended assembly halls and exhibition spaces are colossal, heavily colonnaded structures hewn from slabs of limestone and marble. Some have been repurposed as business hubs, with financial services featuring heavily, while some remain forlornly vacant. Perhaps the Fascist associations affect your judgement – in a sense, how could they not? – but there is something deeply sinister about their brooding presence. Happier memories may come from the fact that some of the edifices bore witness to the 1960 Olympic Games. The restaurant Fungo is perched on top of a striking 'mushroom-shaped' modernist tower that originally held a tank to supply the fire crews on duty at the games with water.

Like this Spomenik, some of th constructions have an undoubted aesthetic appeal if you're it way inclined. The Palazzo della Civiltà Italiana is sometimes known as 'The Square Colosseum'. It has lines of six arches vertically, nine horizontally. These are said to follow the numbers of letters in the words Benito and Mussolini. Clearly a degree of self-aggrandising was all part of the plan to the extent that the tops of each face of the building have extracts from his speeches carved into them. Apparently no one is quite sure of their meaning and context. It's almost as if he was spouting complete crap.

The site is laden with impressive, if stern, statuary and the rows of columns and pedestals certainly echo Roman temple building.

There are also powerful militaristic wall carvings and stupendous mosaics by the Roman futurist Enrico Prampolini. His work is truly sublime and I guess his association with Mussolini's regime is why we haven't really heard of him. It brings to mind the age-old question: can you separate the art and the artist?

Other areas of EUR have been filled in with what might in another setting seem charmless and characterless office blocks, but on the grid system here they seem to chime harmoniously. There are apartment complexes, too, and a surprisingly pleasant tree-lined high street of modern buildings and well-to-do shops including outlets for Dolce & Gabbana and Rolex.

The overall impression you are left with is of a Fascist citadel combined with an ancient place of worship, a Docklands-like business district, a British new town of the late sixties and an upmarket package-holiday resort. It can morph at every corner from the pleasant to the ominous, from welcoming to forbidding, from gentle to brutal. It is an extraordinary place and, within the timeline of the history you're immersed in elsewhere in the Eternal City, it feels like it sprang up yesterday.

Oh, and there did seem to be a lot of people smoking. The popularity of fags might be something to do with the fact that in Rome a packet of twenty costs about €4 or €5 as opposed to upwards of £15 in the UK. As far as I can make out, it is more of an ingrained habit than back home. About 14 per cent of Brits admit to being smokers, which I thought a surprisingly high figure. In Italy, that percentage rises to around 23, which conversely was lower than I expected. I still don't think it constitutes a career, as Arlo speculated. I think they were just taking a well-earned break from banking or possibly smashing bottles.

I didn't try to explain to Arlo that in the seventies laboratory experiments resulted in cigarettes being given to beagles, in case he once again mixed them up with the Beatles.

Bar San Calisto

'Me and Him after the pastry has all gone. Boo.'

Every morning me and Him go to the same place.

I think it's some kind of community centre where old people can go for a chat and a cup of tea.

We share a pastry and He has a little glass with some hot stuff in it. I quite like the taste of the froth off that.

The same people are here every day and some of them stroke me and some aren't interested, which is a bit rude.

We sit there for quite a long time not talking to anybody and not doing anything except watching who comes and goes. You go into a trance after a while unless you see a pigeon.

Sometimes He might have a second little glass with hot stuff in it. I quite like the taste of the froth off that one too.

After that we usually walk round the fountain and then we go back home.

I know this might not sound exciting but me and Him seem to be all right with that. I'm great at just snoozing until something interesting happens. Until then, shall we have some more froth?

He's right. That's the thing about being somewhere for a good while. Not every day needs to be packed with a hectic tourist schedule.

Boketto is a Japanese word meaning 'staring absent-mindedly into the middle distance'. We did that for two hours every morning and considered it time well spent.

But there's more going on here than you might think.

Let's start with the fountain, which is a thirty-second amble round the corner from the Bar San Calisto. It's the Fontana di Santa Maria and is said to be the oldest in Rome, dating back to the eighth century. Bernini had a hand in it but most of the donkey work was undertaken by Donato Bramante. And some builders, obviously.

Our mornings over three months generally followed the same routine. Arlo and I would walk through the fruit and vegetable market and head for the bar. We got to be on nodding terms with some of the local traders. These included a hyperactive greengrocer with more enthusiasm for artichokes than you would think possible and a diminutive Asian florist who seemed to be tending to his copious blooms at all times of day or night. Perhaps he lived in that little booth.

A less amiable presence was the scowling shot-putter of a masseuse who stalked the pavement outside her minuscule parlour. I know what you're thinking. *What sort of massage parlour was this? The remedial kind or the other one?* To be honest, I think it was the former but either way it would have been utterly terrifying. She looked like she would snap you in two without pausing to take the fag out of her mouth.

Bar San Calisto, our regular morning haunt, has been at the centre of Trastevere life since 1969.

At first glance, it's a scruffy and unassuming place. Inside is a long, high wooden bar along one side from where all drinks are served. Opposite is a cash desk with a glass case for pastries and sandwiches. Through an open doorway is a small, linoleum-floored room containing four or five tables. On the walls are snaps of footballing heroes of international, national and local renown. The local football club is called ASD Trastevere Calcio. They play in Serie D. There's a club shop on the Via della Lungaretta if you fancy a replica shirt.

Also adorning the peeling walls of the Bar San Calisto snug are paintings immortalising the humble yet semi-legendary premises and photographs from the life of the owner, Marcello, a smiling, diminutive figure in double denim. The perpetually animated and voluble staff all wear matching T-shirts that list the full range of colourful gelato varieties they have available on the back. These garments are brown. That's so San Calisto. You could never accuse them of being a bit too flashy.

My 'hot stuff' was caffè latte, which was occasionally viewed with suspicion by the not always beaming baristas. I got the distinct impression that they considered it to be a bit of an insult to their proud coffee heritage. A bit like having ice in a prime single malt perhaps.

Well, yes and no. I think if you're a paying customer you should have whatever you want without being given the feeling that you've committed some kind of faux pas, but then I wasn't a local. They didn't care how I felt.

They were always pleased to see Arlo, and such was his love of the foamy latte head that I couldn't order espresso just to please them. He would have looked at me with pure contempt, as if to say:

Have you lost your mind? What about me?

And really, any sense of disapproval from the frowning staff was fleeting. Arlo could have been sulky with me all day.

I'm aware, of course, that I may be guilty of anthropomorphism when it comes to his feelings, but looking through our holiday snaps, there are definitely times when he looks really grumpy.

You couldn't see him in that buggy and not know that he wasn't extremely dis-chuffed. Not quite in the death-glare massage torturer class but certainly pretty miffed.

The coffee cups in Rome are tiny by our standards. All the hot drinks are served in small measures compared to the coffee-chain buckets we've become accustomed to at home. Perhaps that's part of the reason most Romans stay slim. It might be combined with a good diet and quite possibly plenty of tobacco, I suppose, but it's got to help your figure if you don't have half a pint of full-fat milk every time you stop for a brew.

The coffee is also ridiculously cheap at Bar San Calisto. My morning coffee and croissant cost €2. A small beer cost €1.50, which goes some way to explaining the queues out of the door during the afternoon and evening. That same beer cost a euro in the supermarket down the block. Half a euro profit per bottle then, even if the bar bought them at that minimart, which I daresay they don't. Amazing. Sure, they sell a lot of them but the same drink will cost you upwards of €5 almost anywhere else.

At San Calisto the real magic happens outside, though. There is a large, cobbled forecourt full of plastic chairs and small round tables sporting the Peroni logo. That brewery was founded in Vigevano in 1846 and moved to Rome in 1864, and these tables look like they might have been around since that time. Here, every day, from early morning until late into the night, locals gather to drink, chat, chain smoke and mingle with tourists 'in the know'. I say 'in the know' because this isn't a place you'd be immediately drawn to if you were just wandering by. It doesn't look anything special and it is always crowded. You'll always get a seat though. If it's full someone will have moved on by the time you've ordered. During the day at any rate. The Italian habit is to quickly down a shot of treacle-like coffee, roll a fag and then get on your way. Not everyone lingers.

Some do, though, and you get to notice the ever-presents on the cast list. There's an old, heavily lined woman with multiple necklaces who always wears a fresh flower in her hair. Another familiar face is a grande dame sporting an outsized floral headband who starts each day with an ice-cream cone. There's also a middle-aged chap with a scrubby topknot and spectacles that look like swimming goggles. I went every day for twelve weeks and he was never not there. He was even in evidence with three other habitués on one of the extremely rare occasions when it was closed. They were sitting on the otherwise deserted frontage playing cards. This place is at the heart of things even when shut.

One of the *dramatis personae* was an old lad in a flat cap pushing his antiquated bicycle. I never saw him actually ride it. From the pannier on the back he would produce whatever repast he'd decided on that day. Usually it seemed to be a large Tupperware bowl of cold spaghetti, which he would devour voraciously while the Bluetooth speaker taped to his crossbar blasted out music from the eighties even though he looked like he might be in his eighth decade himself. On three separate occasions we were treated to the greatest hits of Fine Young Cannibals. He didn't buy anything from the bar but no one seemed to mind.

On the opposite side of the street is a doorway where a revolving cast of unfortunates spend their days sitting on the step. And yet even these otherwise lost souls seem to be part of San Calisto society. They buy, or someone else buys them, the odd coffee and they can often be seen chatting to Marcello or other locals who linger.

There's often music, too. With bottle in hand as the sun dropped we'd lean against the adjacent crumbling wall where half-torn posters fluttered in the twilight to appreciate a more than adept troupe of jazzateers. In truth, this could be a mixed blessing as you may have the misfortune to encounter the performance during the extended bass solo. Nobody wants that.

And there seems to be a communally accepted code. A set of loose rules and regulations. They don't do table service. Unless they do. For some.

Topknot took money from an old lady to go to the kiosk on the corner of the square to buy her cigarettes. He received two from the packet for his trouble.

On one occasion, a greatly distressed grandmother arrived at the front gate haphazardly driving a greatly distressed Fiat Punto.

After much collective gesticulation and expostulation three regulars borrowed a spanner from behind the bar and fumbled about under the bonnet for about half an hour, forcing all-comers to squeeze round a dented wing to obtain their breakfast. That's very much the San Calisto way.

'Buongiorno. Caffè latte, per favore.'

'Yes, mate. Just as soon as I've drained this oil sump. Cute dog, by the way.'

But in Italian.

The listless hours *boketto*-ing there were some of the most blissful times of our stay.

Arlo would just sit on my knee, accepting cooing attention from his frequent admirers as if it were no more than he deserved. I guess that happens to him quite a lot and so it's just the way he expects life to be. It was part of the whole experience of being in the Eternal City that for part of every day we just let the world wash over us rather than heading determinedly into it. Such was our sense of serenity and contentment that our friends back home alerted us to the appearance of a photograph of Arlo and me on the Instagram page of the well-known Italian blogger and food writer Sophie Minchilli. The caption under the pic read:

'Slow mornings in Rome.'

The posting attracted a lot of adoring comments, many of them including the word 'handsome'.

Relating to whom, do you think?

Bar San Calisto is a café, a pub, a drop-in centre, a meeting place and a community hub.

It is a Trastevere institution. It is a way of life. It is its own little world and out of everything we encountered in Rome, it is the thing I will miss most.

Well, that and the light.

Epilogue by Mark

And so reluctantly, three months having flown by, it was time to leave.

Heading northwest we took a detour to the coast to drop in at Cinque Terre, about an hour from Genoa or Pisa. This translates as 'Five Lands' and consists of a quintuple of truly delightful, brightly hued clusters of traditional buildings crowding the sides of narrow streets leading down to the sea. There is a train every half hour linking them so you can do them all in a day if you've a mind to. Better to take a little more time, though, and traverse one of the rocky paths between different locations, but be warned, while the views are spectacular, it's pretty tough going.

We stayed in Vernazza in a traditional village house with a certain rustic charm. Next to our loo was a sign asking guests not to put 'foreign objects' down it. There was a helpful illustration showing a red cross over a box, a cup and a bottle.

Do people do that? Has that happened after a romantic evening involving champagne?

'Barry, what are you doing in there?'

'I'm trying to get this jeroboam down the toilet.'

A pause.

'You know when I said I loved you a minute or two ago?'

'Yes.'

'I'm wondering about that now.'

Of the five towns, Monterosso al Mare is the biggest and most like a traditional resort with its elegant promenade sweeping around the bay.

Lonely Corniglia sits four hundred steps above its station on a windswept clifftop.

Vernazza, Riomaggiore and Manarola are gaily painted fishing villages, which are idyllic if swamped by trippers during the day. Evening is your best time. Take a bottle, cups and snacks to the rocks by the harbour and watch the sun go down. These are very well-tended places, though, so don't leave any rubbish. Take it home with you. And flush it down the toilet.

Onwards we went into the Mont Blanc Tunnel, which is convenient if expensive: €55 one way. And it's only seven miles long so not even the longest road tunnel in the world. That's the Lærdal Tunnel in Norway, which is twice that length and has a rest area halfway through where you can hold a wedding if you like.

'Barry, you know you asked me to marry you and I said yes?'

'Yes.'

'And then you said we were going to have our big day halfway through a tunnel?'

'Yes.'

'Do I get a say in that?'

Arlo seemed agitated during our subterranean odyssey. He refused to lie down and kept glancing suspiciously at the tunnel lights whizzing by. Whether it was the thunderous roar of the trucks amplified by the concrete walls or an indignation that the trip was costing us more-or-less €8 a mile I couldn't say, but when we emerged into the daylight he happily hunkered down again.

We had reached France, where our next stop was Annecy. It is a beautiful medieval city of cobbled squares, historic buildings and lantern-lit passageways by the side of a lake, with the clear, ice-blue waters of the River Thiou running through its heart. It was very different to Rome. The graffiti was much neater and restricted to bridges and underpasses, the dogs were nicer, people stopped for you at zebra crossings and there were a lot of joggers about. We hadn't seen any of that malarkey in Rome.

Not only is Annecy pretty, it also rather marvellously smells of cheese due to the local love of fondue and raclette. After a long day's drive, I'd rather set my mind on having a massive steak burger and chips but the smell of melting fromage was causing some serious salivation. How amazing then to sit down at Le Zinc à Raoul to find their house burger came with a fondue topping. Some days are just a total win.

Arlo had quite a lot of burger, which helped him get over having his legally required tapeworm treatment earlier in the day. This only involved a visit to a vet, who made him swallow a tablet and then stamped his ludicrously overpriced piece of paper in lieu of a proper passport. Clearly the swallowing of the lozenge was anything but traumatic but he knows a veterinary surgery when he smells one and understands some undignified prodding and manipulation can regularly occur there. His perennially wagging tail was firmly clamped to his backside until we got back out to the car park.

Another day took us back to Calais and the short hop to Folkestone via Le Shuttle.

In a way, it was good to be back in Knutsford where I have everything I need. I'm a home-loving type at heart but that doesn't mean that our stay in Rome wasn't one of the great experiences of my life. It is a place of wonder, romance, beauty, mystery and quite repetitive menu choices. At every turn, you are given a graphic history lesson or confronted by the greatest examples of high art. Every corner looks like a scene from an exquisitely shot film. It is a metropolis that doesn't harass you or rip you off but just embraces you in a world of treasures and touchstones of civilisation. It is, to my mind, the greatest city in the world. I mean, I haven't been to all of them, obviously, but it's the greatest city I know of and I include London and New York in that.

Part of my heart will always lie in Manchester, but even though the Central Library is round and has pillars, it's not the Pantheon, is it?

But it's not the 'big hitters' of the tourist map in Rome that ultimately stay with you. It is just the sense of sitting back and letting the atmosphere seep into you.

I will never forget waking up to the light, taking the 1950s caged lift to the lobby, heaving open the block's gargantuan distressed doors and walking past Mr Khan's Mini-Market. I'll miss the characters like him eking out a living in the Eternal City.

One time when we were in a taxi waiting at the lights, a cheery little old man in a baseball cap and shell suit knocked on the window and tried to sell us a pen, lighter or packet of tissues. The driver told us he had been doing this at the same junction for more than twenty-five years. You've got to admire that kind of resilience and I felt the same about Mr Khan in his *alimentari* shop. He was always open. Every time I went in he greeted me cheerfully as 'my friend, my friend'.

Sometimes there didn't seem to be a customer for quite a while and at these times he sat outside on the step. It didn't look very comfortable. Mr Khan, buy a little chair, my friend.

I wasn't his friend really and his pricing was erratic. A lot of items seemed to cost whatever he thought was about right at the time. He would enter the numbers not into a till but a calculator and then with a big smile present it to you as if that was somehow proof that it was all above board. But you know, so what? If he made a few extra euros from someone passing through then who cares? He was only trying to survive, like the guy at the traffic lights.

Of course, the whole experience had been made even more memorable by having Arlo at my side at all times. Unless I was visiting a forest or an abattoir.

Walking those antiquated streets that patricians, praetorians, plebeians, painters and poets had previously promenaded, it was always comforting to watch the back of his fluffy head bobbing up and down as he trotted amiably onwards to whatever experience awaited us in the next piazza. He never complained by plonking himself on the pavement and refusing to move, and contentedly sat for endless hours, the waft of pancetta drifting across his snout, as we observed Roman life with an Aperol from a kerb-side table. He was the perfect travelling companion. (Bella wasn't bad either, to be fair.)

And I'll look forward to one day coming back to amble past the barber's, the pasta lab, Le Levain bakery, where everything is delicious, traversing Piazza di San Cosimato by the fruit market, crossing the street to avoid the masseuse, turning left at the Legendary Democratic Republic of Rigatoni and circling the Fontana di Santa Maria. Three coins in the fountain? Well, it's the wrong fountain. You need the Trevi, but no, just the two. That means I shall return. For sure. As the third means you will get married in Rome and I'm already hitched, I'll keep the last coin for Bar San Calisto. There I will buy a coffee, pull up a plastic chair next to a scuffed Peroni table and settle in to watch all human life pass by. In the sunshine. With Arlo perched on my knee. There is no better way of spending a euro that I know of in the whole world.

Arrivederci.

Epilogue by Arlo

I'm back in Knutsford now, where I have everything I need.

I go for my walks on The Moor or The Heath or in Tatton Park.

I get treats from Mel and Nadine at the newspaper shop, Ange and Sally at Cranford Café and Harriet and Fiona at The Tea Rooms.

Sometimes I see my friends Bene and Memphis.

I've got my garden to keep clear of squirrels.

I'm back on the corned beef.

I listen to the radio in the mornings and watch TV at night.

Life's great. I don't need to go anywhere else but perhaps I'll travel in the future.

Rome, you say?

Maybe one day.

I hear the Sistine Chapel is amazing.

And no, I won't forget to look up.

Ciao.

'Me and Him walking moodily into the
middle distance. The End.'

Acknowledgements

Heartfelt thanks to James Gurbutt for belief, encouragement and sage advice and to Alice Watkin for meticulous attention to detail. I'm also deeply grateful for the support of the rest of the crack team at Little, Brown: Katya Ellis, Sophie Ellis, Marie Hrynczak, Jane Selley, Celeste Ward-Best and Howard Watson.

As ever, much appreciation to the always supportive Caroline Chignell and Rebecca Ptaszynksi at PBJ Management.

Thanks also to Carlo Forni whose Trastevere apartment was a true home from home.

Lastly, much love to Bella and Arlo – the best travelling companions a man could wish for.

RAISING READERS
Books Build Bright Futures

Dear Reader,

We'd love your attention for one more page to tell you about the crisis in children's reading, and what we can all do.

Studies have shown that reading for fun is the **single biggest predictor of a child's future life chances** – more than family circumstance, parents' educational background or income. It improves academic results, mental health, wealth, communication skills, ambition and happiness.[1]

The number of children reading for fun is in rapid decline. Young people have a lot of competition for their time. In 2024, 1 in 10 children and young people in the UK aged 5 to 18 did not own a single book at home.[2]

Hachette works extensively with schools, libraries and literacy charities, but here are some ways we can all raise more readers:

- Reading to children for just 10 minutes a day makes a difference
- Don't give up if children aren't regular readers – there will be books for them!
- Visit bookshops and libraries to get recommendations
- Encourage them to listen to audiobooks
- Support school libraries
- Give books as gifts

There's a lot more information about how to encourage children to read on our website: **www.RaisingReaders.co.uk**

Thank you for reading.

---

[1] National Literacy Trust, Book Ownership in 2024, November 2024
https://nlt.cdn.ngo/media/documents/Book_ownership_in_2024

[2] OECD. 2021. 21st-century readers: developing literacy skills in a digital world. Paris, France: OECD Publishing.
https://www.oecd.org/en/publications/21st-century-readers_a83d84cb-en.html